TONI MORRISON'S *BELOVED* AS AFRICAN-AMERICAN SCRIPTURE & OTHER ARTICLES ON HISTORY AND CANON

**Hermit Kingdom Studies in
History and Religion 1**

Toni Morrison's Beloved as African-American Scripture & Other Articles on History and Canon

Heerak Christian Kim

The Hermit Kingdom Press
Cheltenham ♦ Seoul ♦ Bangalore ♦ Cebu

TONI MORRISON'S *BELOVED* AS AFRICAN-AMERICAN SCRIPTURE & OTHER ARTICLES ON HISTORY AND CANON

Copyright © 2006 by Heerak Christian Kim

All rights reserved. No part of this book may be reproduced in any form or by any means, electronic or mechanical, including photocopying, recording, or by any information storage and retrieval system (including computer files in any form), without permission in writing from the publisher.

Hardcover: ISBN 1-59689-052-5
Paperback: ISBN 1-59689-053-3
MS E-Book: ISBN 1-59689-054-1

Write-To Address:
The Hermit Kingdom Press
3741 Walnut Street, Suite 407
Philadelphia, PA 19104
United States of America
info@TheHermitKingdomPress.com
* * * * *
Hermit Kingdom
12 South Bridge, Suite 370
Edinburgh, EH1 1DD
Scotland

Library of Congress Cataloging-in-Publication Data

Kim, H. C. (Heerak Christian)
   Toni Morrison's Beloved as African-American scripture & other articles on history and canon / Heerak Christian Kim.
      p. cm. -- (Hermit Kingdom studies in history and religion ; 1)
   ISBN 1-59689-052-5 (alk. paper) -- ISBN 1-59689-053-3 (pbk. : alk. paper)
   1. Christianity and culture. 2. Church history. 3. History--Religious aspects--Christianity. 4. Black theology. 5. Morrison, Toni. Beloved. I. Title. II. Series.
   BR115.C8K548 2006
   230--dc22
                                              2005037762

For my mother in celebration of her 60th birthday in 2006

"The cost of liberty is less than
the price of repression."

W. E. B. Du Bois
Civil-Rights Leader, 1868-1963

Contents

Toni Morrison's *Beloved* as an
African-American Scripture:
A Study of Horror and Fantasy as Genre
Elements in Scripturalization
≈ 1 ≈

Justin Martyr and his
Biblical Epistemology
≈ 46 ≈

Historical Implications of Nestorius and
Cyril's Theological Differences in the
Fifth Century AD
≈ 82 ≈

Gospel of John's Son of Man:
Communal Self-Definition in Motion
≈ 106 ≈

Self-Perception and Group Identity at
Qumran: Hodayot Scrolls as a Key
≈ 132 ≈

Continuity and Discontinuity in
Christian Baptism
≈ 151 ≈

Contents

John Calvin's Views on Government
☞ 182 ☜

Luther's Position on War
☞ 204 ☜

Preface

This book represents over fifteen years of research relating to canon and history. During this period, I have researched wide and far in the humanities and the social sciences with some of the greatest minds in scholarship today in America, Europe, and the Middle East. I am thankful for the wonderful opportunities to research at the professional level at UCLA, Harvard University, Brown University, Hebrew University of Jerusalem, Cambridge University, and Heidelberg University to name a few universities which have given me much intellectual impetus.

I am particularly thankful for the academic year (1995-96) I spent in the State of Israel as one of ten American Raoul Wallenberg Scholars, researching democracy and human rights. My roommate during that academic year was Walid Chamoun, an 1995-96 Raoul Wallenberg Scholar, and I appreciate his perspective on the Middle East which he frequently shared with me. I also benefited greatly from my friendships with other Raoul Wallenberg Scholars that year, such as John Bartlett, Cory Welt, Adina Shoulson, Hillary Coyne, and Jared Genser. Through research and conversation, I came to realize how experiences, particularly in oppressive settings, produce a type of popular or oral text which takes on a form of canon. I was able to think seriously about how such a canon functions in relevant ways in history and human consciousness.

During the 1995-96 year, the Raoul Wallenberg Scholar program allowed me to intern at Jerusalem's Orion Center for the Study of Dead Sea Scrolls and Associated Literature, created that year and headed by Professor Michael Stone of the Hebrew University of Jerusalem with the assistance of Dr. Esther Chazon. There were two interns that year and the other intern was Martina van den Berg. It was a pleasure to work closely with Michael, Esther, and Martina. It provided me with wonderful opportunities to think about the relationship betwen canon and history, particularly in the context of the history of Second Temple Judaism.

I am thankful for many opportunities that I have had since then (and also before then) of thinking about the formation of written and popular canon and their function and influence in society and history.

I hope to continue creative research into and critical thinking about the question of history

Preface

and canon, and I plan to make major contributions in the scientific understanding of human experience and social consciousness.

I hope that all of my learning, experience, and training will help advance knowledge and betterment of humanity.

Toni Morrison's *Beloved* as
African-American Scripture
& Other Articles on History and Canon

Toni Morrison's *Beloved* as an African-American Scripture: A Study of Horror and Fantasy as Genre Elements in Scripturalization[1]

Understanding the genre is an important way of understanding a literature, a composition, and elements in a work of art. Horror and fantasy are genre and focusing on their nature as genre is helpful for understanding the literature that fall into that genre. However, it is important to recognize that genre categories are not static; one genre (or more) can function as element(s) in another genre. Understanding this possibility and, more importantly, recognizing the applicability of this principle is crucial for understanding the nature of literature, its function, and its value. There are several ways to approach this, but perhaps the most fruitful way of examining this principle is found in the study of scripture as genre. I would argue that scripture is a genre that

---

[1] I would like to thank Professor Vincent Wimbush of Claremont Graduate University for reading the complete paper and commenting on it. And I am particularly grateful for his insights on race and ethnicity which he frequently imparted to me in conversations.

incorporates horror and fantasy elements with a view to preserving past memories important to a community and to create a constructively ordered present identity of the individuals of the community.[2] In this regard, I would argue that Toni Morrison's *Beloved* is a type of African-American scripture.[3]

Before diving into discussing Toni Morrison's *Beloved*, it is important to spend some time examining the genre of scripture in relation to the elements of horror and

---

[2] Scripture and ritual are often linked. Scripture can guide ritual, for instance. It is interesting, therefore, to note the definition of ritual provided by H. Nigel Thomas. He writes: "Before discussing specific rituals in selected Afro-American novels, we need to define what is meant by ritual. .... In this chapter ritual refers to those forms of behavior devised by a people over a long period of time to reinforce the key values of their culture and to promote social harmony and individual and group confidence. This definition implies that ritual is a way of ordering the chaos of existence or a way of programming the individual within the society so that he or she does not fall victim to that chaos" (H. Nigel Thomas, *From Folklore to Fiction: A Study of Folk Heroes and Rituals in the Black American Novel* <New York: Greenwood Press, 1988>, p. 111). It is interesting to note that his definition corresponds to the reality of *Beloved* as an African-American scripture as shown in this paper.

[3] Clarence Major writes: "Writing poems and novels is also a way of inventing answers" (Clarence Major, *The Dark and Feeling: Black American Writers and Their Work* <New York: The Third Press, 1974>, p. 18).

fantasy. What is horror? Horror seems fairly easy to define at first sight. One may say that horror is something that gives a shock value. Thus, horror as genre is literature that shocks. However, the definition of horror using "shock" is grossly inadequate because many things can be shocking. For instance, a shock can come from disgust. Take, for example, watching a boy swallow a goldfish can be shocking. It is possible to say, however, that one is shocked because one is disgusted. How can someone swallow a living thing? How can someone swallow a pet? The shock can be due to elements that may not relate to horror. Thus, the mere shock value does not indicate the intrinsic horror nature of an episode or literature.

But consider this. Let us say that the goldfish suddenly started to grow to an enormous size and swallowed the boy. One can say that he is shocked by that. The same term of "shock" is used but the meaning is quite different. In fact, the way that the word "shock" is used in this context points to horror. What is the difference? The shock involved in watching a boy being swallowed by a goldfish that becomes enormous induces fear. There is a fear at the enlarged goldfish that you just saw swallow a boy could swallow you as well. It is this essential ingredient of fear (potentially vicarious) that attributes the episode with horror. Horror literature is one that captures the fear and helps the reader experience that fear even for a moment.

This is the reason why the movie *Jaws* (1975) was effective as a horror film. This movie directed by Steven Spielberg is set in a peaceful town called Amity. The town could be a typical nice town and the name reinforces that image. In fact, you could be living in a town like this. A young woman, Christine 'Chrissie' Watkins (played by Susan Backlinie), takes a swim and is attacked and killed by a great white shark. This is shocking and induces fear because one can imagine that this can happen to him. What happened to Amity can happen in any coastal town. Thus, in describing horror films, Kendall R. Phillips writes: "Rather, these films connect to existing cultural drifts and directions in such peculiarly poignant ways as to be recognized as somehow 'true.'"[4] Horror as genre induces fear with the recognized possibility of actual or vicarious participation and that is what defines the genre.

Because fear is the dominant characteristic of the horror genre, it is not surprising that horror often becomes associated with evil. When a person goes around in a rampage of killing, one calls him evil. The attribution of "evil" is due to the fact that it

---

[4] Kendall R. Phillips, *Projected Fears: Horror Films and American Culture* (Westport: Praeger Publishers, 2005), p. 5.

induces fear that anyone can potentially be a victim. There is a fearful recognition of one's vicarious identity and potential for active participation in the victim's experience. In other words, horror as genre speaks to what Phillips refers to as "collective nightmares."[5]   Thus, Paul Oppenheimer writes: "Evil, no matter how one wishes to define it, must in fact begin with criminality, and go on from there."[6] Criminality can be seen as potential for violence in a way that trespasses a person's safety or safety zone. For instance, people are afraid of being attacked in their homes in their sleep. Thus, when they see someone trespassing a person's personal property to carry out an hostile attack, they are shocked with fear. They experience fear through vicarious participation in the criminal act and they are afraid of potentially being the victim of such a criminality. Such fear of trespass can be seen as enhancing the horror factor of Vampire stories. Count Dracula can take the form of a bat and fly in through a window to trespass on a sleeping victim. The criminality of the whole process speaks to the collective fears about personal safety and safety zones.

---

[5] Phillips, p. 3.
[6] Paul Oppenheimer, *Evil and the Demonic: A New Theory of Monstrous Behavior* (New York: New York University Press, 1996), p. 3.

The fear of the criminal trespass of one's personal space and safety zone relates to the identification as evil efforts to control those realms. Oppenheimer writes regarding a type of "criminal trespass" of personal space of speech: "Clearly, it is one's very powers of speech that the figures bent on evil wishes to destroy, on the correct assumption that to deprive his victims of language is to deprive them of their very minds, brains, capacities for emotion, for action."[7] In this regard, agents of evil often act on behalf of evil entities, such as evil nations that trespass one's personal space and safety zones, sometimes in rabidly violent ways. Oppenheimer writes: "In countries as diverse as the former German Democratic Republic, Poland, Russia and Romania, a utopian vocabulary was revealed as a shabby camouflage for an empirically evil barbarism."[8] What makes the trespass of personal space and safety zones more evil is the intentioned effort to destroy memory and historical connectedness. Oppenheimer states: "Implicit in this loss of language is the more poisonous issue of the loss of memory. Memory disappears quickly in those kingdoms. Its annihilation is actively sought. One realizes, therefore, that any quest for an evil reality links up with insentient neatness to a quest for historical

---

[7] Oppenheimer, p. 6.
[8] Oppenheimer, p. 173.

amnesia."[9] Criminal trespass of personal space and safety zones can reach into deep-seated fears regarding existence and being. Oppenheimer's assessment of evil encroaching upon one's personal space and safety zones, which induces personal and collective fear and is meant to destroy a person's connectedness to the past, is relevant for understanding Marie Hélène Huet's understanding of horror. Huet describes *Frankenstein* as "a tale of disrupted filiation."[10] In a sense, Frankenstein embodied the fear of becoming disconnected to the past and, thereby, ending of the civilization. Huet writes that *Frankenstein* represents "a literal reproduction of the theory of *emboîtement* or *encasement*, the theory that posited that all future generations were contained in the seed of our first parents and that there would come a time when the last man or woman would be born."[11] Horror, therefore, is integrally connected with evil that seems to trespass personal space and safety zones and instils fear for self-preservation and corporate existence.

Like horror, fantasy (or "the fantastic") is a genre. Although it is possible to find some shared characteristics between

---

[9] Oppenheimer, p. 175.
[10] Marie Hélène Huet, *Monstrous Imagination* (Cambridge: Harvard University Press, 1993), p. 142.
[11] Huet, pp. 142-143.

horror and fantasy, there are key differences. One of the sometimes shared qualities that indicate this reality is the element of fear. Fear is integral to defining the genre of horror, but it is not for the genre of fantasy. Tzvetan Todorov writes: "Fear is often linked to the fantastic, but it is not a necessary condition of the genre."[12] It is further enlightening to point out that horror is defined by fear, whether the fear inducing element is realistic or not realistic. For instance, it would be unrealistic for the goldfish to suddenly increase in size and swallow a human being. However, the fact is that an enlarged goldfish swallowing someone may conjure up other associated fears – for instance, of being swallowed up in a fierce storm or in a flood. On a general level it may conjure up fears of mortality which seems to characterize humanity. But it is not only the fantastic kind of fear that characterizes horror. Horror can be real and realistic. A shark eating a human being who is swimming is not out of the realm of reality. A mass murderer going around killing people is not out of the experience of reality. However, they are certainly belonging to horror. In other words, whether fear inducing element is real or imaginary does not matter in determining

---

[12] Tzvetan Todorov, *The Fantastic: A Structural Approach to a Literary Genre*, trans. by Richard Howard (Ithaca: Cornell University Press, 1975), p. 35.

the genre of horror. It is different with the genre of fantasy, or "the fantastic."

Rosemary Jackson's book, *Fantasy: The Literature of Subversion*, is helpful for understanding the nature of the genre of the fantastic. Jackson writes: "Fantasy has always provided a clue to the limits of a culture, by foregrounding problems of categorizing the 'real' and of the situation of the self in relation to that dominant notion of 'reality.'"[13] In other words, Fantasy must push the bounds of reality. Thus, fantasy cannot be real or realistic.

This can be understood on two levels: composer/storyteller on the one hand and reader/listener/viewer on the other hand. If a person is writing a fantasy story or making a fantasy movie, he must consciously work to push the bounds of reality as it exists and as it is recognized. In other words, he cannot write in the realm of what is recognized as real or realistic and call it fantasy. An example will illustrate what is being stated. If someone writes about cashing his frequent flier miles to be a passenger on a spaceship adventure to visit the moon, it would not be fantasy. Virgin Atlantic Airways has started such a program (albeit with a view to the future). Such a story in the year 2005 would not be a fantasy because it is a part of the reality of 2005. However,

---

[13] Rosemary Jackson, *Fantasy, the Literature of Subversion* (London: Methuen, 1981), p. 52.

had this story been composed in the year 1005, it would have been fantasy. It would have been contrary to the reality as they understood it and experienced it.

In a sense, therefore, fantasy is what it is on account of its relation to the reality as experienced or perceived at the time. It is intrinsically relative in nature. In other words, it is the current reality that defines what is fantasy by its relation to it. Jackson writes: "A literary fantasy is produced within, and determined by, its social context. Though it might struggle against the limits of this context, after being articulated upon that very struggle, it cannot be understood in isolation from it."[14] What a society understands collectively as reality, therefore, defines what is fantasy. Thus, it is not difficult to see that understanding of reality could differ from society to society.

Different societies understand reality differently on account of various factors. If one visits a secluded tribe area in South America, where the tribe members have never been exposed to the news of landing on the moon or America's space program, then the story of a person flying in a spaceship to the moon may appear like a fantasy. The secluded tribe of South America has not been exposed to technological advancements that most Americans take for granted. In other words, what Americans

---

[14] Jackson, p. 3.

consider reality is not considered reality by some other societies on account of their experiences and history.

Taking this idea further, it is possible to show that some societies differ from other societies on account of their chosen realities. In other words, some societies choose to delineate what is real or not based on their religious, social, intellectual, personal, or cultural belief system. For instance, consider this case. In Charismatic Christian settings, it is understood as reality that God still communicates through prophecy. On the contrary, an Atheist will deem it out of the realm of reality for a non-existent supernatural, divine being to communicate. What is reality for one would be deemed fantasy by the other. This distinction is possible not only on the individual level but on a societal level, where different societies are prefigured along certain mores, belief system, historical experience, and cultural practices. Jackson writes: "Definitions of what can 'be,' and images of what cannot be, obviously undergo considerable historical shifts. Non-secularized societies hold different beliefs from secular cultures as to what constitutes 'reality.' Presentations of otherness are imagined and interpreted differently."[15] It may be possible to say that the reality is in the eye of the beholder.

---

[15] Jackson, p. 23.

Perhaps, it is this subjective element in fantasy that causes Todorov to discuss the genre of fantasy in partial and structural terms in his book, *The Fantastic: A Structural Approach to a Literary Genre*. Even in regards to term usage, Todorov prefers to use the term "the fantastic" to describe the genre of fantasy. It focuses on the elemental dynamics of fantasy in literature. Todorov writes:

> The fantastic occupies the duration of this uncertainty. Once we choose one answer or the other, we leave the fantastic for a neighboring genre, the uncanny or the marvelous. The fantastic is that hesitation experienced by a person who knows only the law of nature, confronting an apparent supernatural event.[16]

Todorov, in a sense, reduces the genre of fantasy to an element or a series of elements that invokes hesitation.

Todorov's definition of the fantastic as genre is difficult precisely because he seems to confuse genre as traditionally understood as a corpus of literature or a whole of literature with an episode within a literature. This confusion is not helped by his

---

[16] Todorov, p. 25.

example of "the fantastic" as found in The Saragossa Manuscript.[17] A man makes love to two beautiful women the night before only to wake up to corpses of two dead men. Todorov illustrates that the fantastic is found in the character before he realizes in the morning that there are two dead men with him. That is the reality; what happened, or is imagined, is the fantasy. In a sense, the fantastic is resolved for the reader as well when realizing the reality that the character wakes up with two dead men. Thus, Todorov reduces the genre of the fantastic to an episode. Supposedly, we are left to infer that a literature is a fantasy if it has the fantastic in it.

Adding greater confusion to Todorov's description of the fantastic as genre is his insistence that what he calls the genre of the fantastic can differ from the character in the story and the reader who is reading the story. For Todorov, duality necessarily exists because the text containing the character who may be experiencing the fantastic in the narrative itself is read by the reader who may have a different understanding of the fantastic. Todorov writes:

> The fantastic, as we have seen, lasts only as long as a certain hesitation: a hesitation common to reader and

---

[17] Todorov, p. 43.

> character, who must decide whether or not what they perceive derives from 'reality' as it exists in the common opinion. At the story's end, the reader makes a decision even if the character does not; he opts for one solution or the other, and thereby emerges from the fantastic.[18]

In other words, it is possible for the character in the story to remain in the realm of the fantastic, while the reader decides that the story has escaped fantasy into reality.

An example will further illustrate the difficulty of Todorov's seeming confusion. If a person in America today writes a story about a tribe in South America which does not have exposure to America and has never heard of people taking a spaceship to go visit the moon, then in the story's narrative, the tribe members would be experiencing the fantastic. The modern-day American reader reading the story would know that there are spaceships that fly to the moon, so that the element would not be fantastic at all. Of course, in the example of the spaceship there is no hesitation. In Todorov's lingo, because there is no hesitation, there is no fantasy for the reader. However, for the character in the story bound in its narrative

---

[18] Todorov, p. 41.

context, it would be different. The character may assume that there is no spaceship that flies to the moon, so that episode would be fantasy for him.

It is easy to see the problem arising from Todorov's discourse. What does it mean to say that a literature is fantasy? Todorov's approach is not helpful for answering traditional questions of genre. But it is in his creative, structuralist approach that we find something that is far more useful than identifying a work of literature as fantasy. Todorov has succeeded in deconstructing literature to its elemental level. He has even stripped those elements that could be fantastic of their stagnant identity. The reader is involved and participates in the determining of the genre element of the fantastic. In fact, it is the reader who is wholly needed for identification of the fantastic. Todorov writes:

> First of all, we have given a definition of the genre: the fantastic is based essentially on a hesitation of the reader – a reader who identifies with the character – as to the nature of an uncanny event. This hesitation may be resolved so that the event is acknowledged as reality, or so that the event is identified

as the fruit of imagination or the result of an illusion; in other words, we may decide that the event *is* or is *not*.[19]

Todorov gives full power to the reader in determining the genre of the text. The composer is helpless to influence the verdict of the reader. Although Todorov's subjective emphasis may seem to complicate identifying the fantastic, his conclusions are fundamentally sound in light of perception of reality determining the genre of fantasy.

Since what is real in one society may seem unreal or unrealistic in another culture, what may not be fantasy for one society could be fantasy for another society. In fact, the only determinant of what would be fantasy is the reader, bound by his society's discourse and perception on reality. It is, therefore, more useful to study episodes that could be fantastic and decide whether they are fantasy or not for the reader in his societal context. Thus, despite the confusion and difficulties that seem to arise from separating the literature from the reader, Todorov's contribution to understanding the element of the fantastic is significant. One may argue that by argument of synecdoche, it is possible to infer that literature with fantastic element is fantasy in genre.

---

[19] Todorov, p. 157.

For our purposes, what is important is that Todorov's breaking down the fantastic as an element that is dependent on reader verdict is helpful for our discussion on scripture. I would argue that scripture necessarily requires horror and fantasy elements that are a part (or a picture) of their genres. In essence, therefore, I would define scripture as a genre that incorporates horror and fantasy elements with a view to preserving past memories important to a community and creating a present identity of the individuals of the community.

It is, however, important to remember the distinction between the genre element of fantasy and that of horror for structural analysis purposes. As I have stated earlier, horror necessarily requires fear. The genre requirement would translate into elemental characteristic of horror. It is this genre characteristic of horror that operates in scripture. In other words, it is the trait that defines the horror element in scripture. Like horror, fantasy is an essential element of scripture and this element, too, points to its genre characteristics. Fantasy, or "the fantastic," is that element that is out of the realm of what is perceived to be real or realistic. Of course, in Todorov's language, this can be described as "hesitation." The hesitation can be short-lived or more permanent. For genre element of fantasy to operate in scripture, it must cause a

17

hesitation as to the reality of its nature. The fantastic solicits the question: Could that really happen? Such elements of the fantastic exist in scripture as it is the case with horror. In fact, scripture is scripture because it uses elements of horror and fantasy in order to preserve past memories important to a community and to strengthen the present identity of the community for whom it is written. In this regard, I would argue that Toni Morrison's *Beloved* is a type of African-American scripture. In a sense, therefore, Toni Morrison's scripturalizing *Tendenz* is found in the purpose of her text infused strategically with horror and fantasy elements to achieve her goals to remember the African-American past and preserve the African-American community.

And Toni Morrison is effective in the use of horror and fantasy in her book, *Beloved*. I will first examine Morrison's use of horror and then examine her use of fantasy. Of course, the two elements intersect at many points and may seem at times to be integrally linked. This may be so, but for the purposes of understanding how the two genre elements of horror and fantasy operate in Morrison's writing, it is useful to discuss horror and fantasy separately.

So, what horror elements are found in *Beloved*? There are many horror elements found in Morrison's novel, but the unifying theme or horror element is slavery.[20] Terry Otten writes: "There is no question, of course, that slavery and its proponents are the consummate evil in the novel...."[21] Slavery, in fact, is horror and all horror elements flow from it. In fact, each horror element points to the horror of slavery and, in a sense, all the horror elements work together to emphasize the horror of slavery. This is clearly evident in the greatest horror in the story, which, of course, is the story of how Sethe killed her own baby daughter, who came back as Beloved. It is a shock to learn that the woman expected most to love her child is the one who killed her in cold blood. This is the fear factor that functions as horror in the novel.

---

[20] The fact of slavery impedes the understanding not only of the self, but also of national identity, which is perhaps the most important quantifiable identity in modern times. Ralph Elliston writes regarding this struggle of the African-American community in history: "Obviously the experiences of Negroes – slavery, the gruelling and continuing fight for full citizenship enforced alienation which constantly knifes into our natural identification with our country – have not been that of white Americans" (Ralph Ellison, "Twentieth-Century Fiction and the Black Mask of Humanity," *Images of the Negro in American Literature*, ed. Seymour L. Gross and John Edward Hardy (Chicago: The University of Chicago Press, 1966, pp. 115-131>, p. 115).

[21] Terry Otten, *The Crime of Innocence in the Fiction of Toni Morrison* (Columbia: University of Missouri Press, 1989), p. 82.

This idea is emphasized by Morrison in the voice of Denver, Sethe's daughter. Denver muses: "I love my mother but I know she killed one of her own daughters, and tender as she is with me, I'm scared of her because of it."[22] The horror of what Sethe has done is emphasized in placing blame for Sethe's sons running away on the fact that she killed her daughter. Denver affirms: "She missed killing my brothers and they knew it. They told me die-witch! Stories to show me the way to do it, if ever I needed to." [23] Furthermore, the horror of Sethe's killing of her daughter is stressed in Paul D leaving Sethe "that very day"[24] that he found out through Stamp Paid, who showed him the past newspaper clip about Sethe's murder. The fact that it happened close to two decades ago did not minimize the horror.

As great as the horror of a mother killing her child, the greater horror for Toni Morrison is slavery. In fact, the horror of the horrendous murder emphasizes the magnitude of the evil of slavery and the fear that it caused. Years after the murder, Sethe justifies the murder. Sethe defends her actions to Paul D when he discovers the murder and confronts her. She says that she was right to kill her child because it did not allow for the

---

[22] Toni Morrison, *Beloved: A Novel* (New York: Vintage Books, 2004), p. 242.
[23] Morrison, *Beloved*, p. 242.
[24] Morrison, *Beloved*, p. 199.

slave owner to possess her. Sethe states: "They ain't at Sweet Home. Schoolteacher ain't got em."[25] Sethe emphasizes that her action was justified because slavery would have been far worse for her child than death. Sethe proclaims: "It's my job to know what is and to keep them away from what I know is terrible. I did that."[26] The justification for having killed her own daughter is reiterated in the novel in the voice of Sethe:

> Beloved, she my daughter. She mine. See. She come back to me of her own free will and I don't have to explain a thing. I didn't have time to explain before because it had to be done quick. Quick. She had to be safe and I put her where she would be. …. I'll explain to her, even though I don't have to. Why I did it. How if I hadn't killed her she would have died and that is something I could not bear to happen to her. When I explain it she'll understand, because she understands everything already.[27]

---

[25] Morrison, *Beloved*, p. 194.
[26] Morrison, *Beloved*, p. 194.
[27] Morrison, *Beloved*, p. 236.

For Sethe, her daughter coming under the slave-owner's authority was like being killed. The horror of her murder was nothing compared to the horrors of slavery. Gurleen Grewal describes Sethe's killing of her daughter in positive terms and states that Sethe "dares to claim her children as her own property instead of the slaveowner's. If the master could subject the slave children to slow 'social death,' the mother could release them through physical death."[28]

The question remains if Morrison depicts Sethe's act as a positive act or not. Otten argues that despite the horrors of slavery, Morrison took the position that *Kindermord* was immoral and objects to it.[29] Grewal, however, disagrees and states: "Morrison also portrays the mother's deed as a heroic act of resistance, one among many that constituted the quotidian experience of slaves."[30] Grewal's proof is in the fact that there are other acts of *Kindermord* in the novel. Ella, a woman perceived as good in the novel, who helps Stamp Paid with the Underground Railroad, did not take care of the baby born to her from rape by white slave owners. The end result was that

---

[28] Gurleen Grewal, *Circles of Sorrow, Lines of Struggle* (Baton Rouge: Louisiana State University Press, 1998), p. 97.
[29] Otten, pp. 82-83.
[30] Grewal, p. 101.

the baby died five days after birth. Sethe's mother also abandoned the children born from rape by white slave owners. She only kept Sethe, who was conceived by an African-American father.[31] Grewal's proof is convincing in light of the fact that there is no real narrative[32] condemnation of these acts. And although seeming to state that Morrison comdemns *Kindermord*, elsewhere Otten seems to argue in another way. This is implicitly visible in the general description of Morrison's worldview. Otten writes: "Certainly Morrison understands well what the romantics learned long ago, that in a society operated by an oppressive order, not to sin in the conventional sense perpetuates an immoral justice. In such a world innocence is itself a sign of guilt, because it signals a degenerate acquiescence."[33] It seems that even Otten implicitly recognizes that Morrison's worldview would sanction Sethe's act. Certainly, the novel pushes this kind of vision.

Further convincing of the idea that novel portrays Sethe killing her child in a positive light is found in the resolution of

---

[31] Grewal, p. 101.

[32] This is significant in light of what Valerie Smith points out: "Morrison suggests that the narrative process leads to self-knowledge because it forces an acceptance of the past" (Valerie Smith, *Self-Discovery and Authority in Afro-American Narrative* <Cambridge: Harvard University Press, 1987>, p. 122).

[33] Otten, p. 4.

the novel. Sethe is accepted back into the community. When Sethe is being persecuted by Beloved, the African-American women in the community gather together to save her. Despite the fact that Sethe killed the child who was now torturing her, the women in the community agree that they need to save Sethe. Ella argues: "No, and the children can't just up and kill the mama."[34] So, thirty women were organized to rescue Sethe and go over to her house.[35] And they carried through the saving of Sethe at a risk to themselves. In a sense, this was a way of the women to repent for the way they treated Sethe while condemning her of killing her baby. They came to realize that the greater evil was slavery. The narrative in *Beloved* supports this: "The Society managed to turn infanticide and the cry of savagery around, and build a further case for abolishing slavery."[36] In a sense, therefore, the women who came to rescue Sethe came to see her side of the story and accept it. Indeed, a story of mother killing her child is shocking; however, Morrison emphasizes that what was more shocking than that was slavery. In other words, greater fear than being killed by someone who loves you the most is being enslaved. That was true horror.

---

[34] Morrison, *Beloved*, p. 301.
[35] Morrison, *Beloved*, p. 303.
[36] Morrison, *Beloved*, p. 307.

Even Paul D, who levelled the direct criticism at Sethe previously comes to accept Sethe's views. Paul comes back unconditionally and in his return does not condemn Sethe. In fact, Paul D comes back singing a love song of eternal love. Paul D sings: "Love that woman till you go stone blind, / Stone blind stone blind, / Sweet Home gal make you lose your mind."[37] Paul D's presence provide the message of a happily-ever-after. It is a fairytale ending despite the fact that Sethe had killed her child. In fact, the happy ending with Sethe winning her man for happily-ever-after is an affirmation that her deed was righteous in light of the circumstances and in view of the horror of slavery. The affirmation of Sethe and her innate righteousness is further emphasized towards the end of the novel in the words of Paul D:

> "Sethe," he says, "me and you, we got more yesterday than any body. We need some kind of tomorrow."
> He leans over and takes her hand. With the other he touches her face. "You your best thing, Sethe. You are." His holding fingers are holding hers.

---

[37] Morrison, *Beloved*, p. 310.

"Me? Me?"[38]

True horror was slavery and it is something that all should be willing to understand. Sethe's hands that killed her baby not only did not deny Sethe as a wonderful woman, but, in fact, it also affirmed her as a wonderful woman. She resisted slavery in a brave way. The logic of Morrison's novel makes sense in light of the unethical practice of the majority dominant group in subjecting Sethe and others to slavery. Wendy Harding and Jacky Martin encapsulate this idea:

> As an artistic mouthpiece for her community, Morrison reconsiders the validity of myths ... in order to counter two insinuating dangers that have always beset and are still threatening the black community: first, the dangers of destruction, the constant risk, instigated in slavery times and extended in more insidious forms in contemporary society, of being exposed to violence because one does not conform to the norm of majority criteria; and, second, the danger of ideological acculturation

---

[38] Morrison, *Beloved*, p. 322.

attending the unmitigated hegemony of the dominant group.[39]

The dominant myth is often validated at the cost of the dominated group. This is what Morrison's *Beloved* opposes. Morrison effectively uses the element of horror in *Beloved*. But contrary to the superficial surface reading, the greatest horror is not a mother killing her child. True horror is the oppression of slavery,[40] which included infliction of physical pain, degradation, and break-up of community and corporate identity. Thus, in the novel Stamp Paid defends Sethe's action by saying: "She ain't crazy. She love those children. She was trying to out-hurt the hurter."[41] This horror of slavery is what Morrison emphasizes in her novel. It is horror that conscientious readers can identify with.

---

[39] Wendy Harding and Jacky Martin, *A World of Difference: An Inter-Cultural Study of Toni Morrison's Novels* (Westport: Greenwood Press, 1994), p. 113.

[40] Brian Finney writes: "Ultimately the novel is about the haunting of the entire Black race by the inhuman experience of slavery, about the damage it did to their collective psyche..." (Brian Finney, "Temporal Defamiliarization in Toni Morrison's *Beloved*," *Critical Essays on Toni Morrison's Beloved*, ed. Barbara H. Solomon <New York: G. K. Hall & Co., 1998, pp. 104-116>, p. 115).

[41] Morrison, *Beloved*, p. 276.

Morrison effectively uses the genre element of horror to preserve important past memory of the African-American community and to help the present identity[42] of the community. Thus, Morrison uses horror as a device in the creation of a type of African-American scripture. Likewise, Morrison adeptly utilizes the genre element of fantasy to achieve a similar effect.

The major fantastic genre element in *Beloved* is obviously Beloved. Beloved is first introduced in the novel as a nameless ghost. Denver tells Paul D: "We have a ghost in here."[43] Denver and her mother Sethe both recognize the ghost as the spirit of the dead baby, whose tombstone read, "Beloved."[44] However, the name of the ghost is not understood as Beloved in the beginning of the book. This is clearly evident in the way the novel starts: "124 was spiteful. Full of a baby's venom. The women in the house knew it and so did the

---

[42] Freedom to define identity became important for African-Americans. Donald A. Petesch describes the idea of "freedom" for the community: "Increasingly, too, it has meant freedom from the definitions of others. In this form it merges with the struggle for identity/self, from which it has never, in any of its forms, been wholly free" (Donald A. Petesch, *A Spy in the Enemy's Country: The Emergence of Modern Black Literature* <Iowa City: University of Iowa Press, 1989>, p. 51).

[43] Morrison, *Beloved*, p. 15.

[44] Morrison, *Beloved*, p. 5.

children. For years each put up with the spite in his own way, but by 1873 Sethe and her daughter Denver were its only victims."[45] The fact that the unnamed ghost is identified with the number of the house emphasizes the idea that the house is haunted by this ghost. Apparently, people don't visit the house, leaving Sethe and Denver alone in the haunted house. Denver complains: "I can't live here. I don't know where to go or what to do but I can't live here. Nobody speaks to us. Nobody comes by. Boys don't like me. Girls don't either."[46] Paul D, the man who enters their house and their lives, recognizes the negative in the fantastic as represented in the ghost and tries to comfort them. Paul D says: "Leave off, Sethe. It's hard for a young girl living in a haunted house. That can't be easy."[47] In accord with Todorov's criterion for the fantastic, the ghost captures the hesitation on the part of the reader.

The fact that the ghost seems to have almost human attributes contributes to the hesitation that the reader feels in deciding whether the whole episode would fit better in the genre of the uncanny or the marvelous, to use Todorov's language.[48] Paul D describes the ghost: "But sad, your mama

---

[45] Morrison, *Beloved*, p. 3.
[46] Morrison, *Beloved*, p. 17.
[47] Morrison, *Beloved*, p. 17.
[48] Todorov, p. 25.

said. Not evil."[49] Denver also describes the ghost as if it were a person: "Rebuked. Lonely and rebuked."[50] In fact, Sethe states plainly: "It's just a baby."[51] The ghost's human-like nature is most evident when Paul D drives the ghost away from the house.[52] The narrative of the novel relates the departure of the ghost as if a friend of Denver has departed: "Now her mother was upstairs with the man who had gotten rid of the only other company she had. Denver dipped a bit of bread into the jelly. Slowly, methodically, miserably she ate it."[53] But despite the anthropomorphic language, the ghost was the spirit of the dead child. The unnamed child ghost with human-like qualities certainly adds a fantastic dimension to the story.

The unnamed ghost further functions to add to the fantasy of the story as it becomes hypostasized[54] into a grown woman,

---

[49] Morrison, *Beloved*, p. 15.
[50] Morrison, *Beloved*, p. 16.
[51] Morrison, *Beloved*, p. 16.
[52] Morrison, *Beloved*, p. 22.
[53] Morrison, *Beloved*, p. 23.
[54] Elizabeth B. House believes that "evidence throughout the book suggests that the girl is not a supernatural being of any kind but simply a young woman who has suffered the horrors of slavery" (Elizabeth B. House, "Toni Morrison's Ghost: The Beloved Who Is Not Beloved," *Critical Essays on Toni Morrison's Beloved*, ed. Barbara H. Solomon <New York: G. K. Hall & Co., 1998, pp. 117-126>, p. 117). However, House does not provide much

named Beloved.[55] The cast-away bodiless spirit has returned with a body. And her return seems to be shrouded in fantasy. The narrative describes:

> A fully dressed woman walked out of the water. She barely gained the dry bank of the stream before she sat down and leaned against a mulberry tree. All day and all night, she sat there, her head resting on the trunk in a position abandoned enough to crack the brim in her straw hat. Everything hurt but her lungs most of all. Sopping wet and breathing shallow she spent those hours trying to negotiate the weight of her eyelids. The day breeze blew her dress dry; the night wind wrinkled it. Nobody saw her emerge or came accidentally by. If they had, chances are they would have hesitated before approaching her. Not because she was wet, or dozing or had what sounded

---

evidence to support her claims. And the consensus upholds the idea that Beloved is clearly the ghost of the murdered girl who took human form.

[55] Morrison, *Beloved*, p. 62.

like asthma, but because amid all that she was smiling.[56]

The whole description borders on the fantastic because it seems out of the ordinary. It is difficult to picture a grown woman coming out of the water fully clothed as if that were normal. Further contributing to the element of the fantastic is the fact that the account seems to describe a type of birth of a baby. This grown women who is fully clothed is almost like a baby who is just born. She was inside the mother's tomb – inside water – and now she is out. The new born baby would lie day and night and lean on whatever she was placed on. The baby would have her eyelids closed in sleep for most of the time. The wet diaper would be dried by day's breeze. The dried diaper would be wrinkled on the baby's person during the night from wear. And despite all that's going on, baby would be thought to smile.

    The attributes of a new born baby is not confined to the initial narrative. Traits of a baby seem to color the description of Beloved, adding to the element of the fantastic. For instance, the narrative describes Beloved's baby-like skin: "She had new skin, lineless and smooth, including the

---

[56] Morrison, *Beloved*, p. 60.

knuckles of her hands."[57] Even her feet had baby-like skin: "Sethe saw that her feet were like her hands, soft and new."[58] The baby imagery is encouraged explicitly by the use of the word "baby" in the description: "Her skin was flawless except the three vertical scratches on her forehead so fine and think they seemed at first like hair, baby hair before it bloomed and roped into the masses of black yarn under her hat." [59] Furthermore, Denver taking care of Beloved is like taking care of a baby. Denver cautiously watched Beloved sleep, listened to her sleeping sound, and even changed Beloved's underwear that had been sullied, not unlike changing a dirty diaper.[60] Thus, Otten comments: "Though the stranger is no longer a child but the twenty-year-old she would have been had she lived, Beloved assumes the person of a newborn."[61]

Besides the imagery of a baby that seems to characterize the grown woman who appears mysteriously, there is another factor that contributes to the element of fantasy surrounding Beloved; namely, the element of non-recognition. Despite what happened before and the perennial acknowledgment of the baby ghost who was buried in a gravesite

---

[57] Morrison, *Beloved*, p. 61.
[58] Morrison, *Beloved*, p. 62.
[59] Morrison, *Beloved*, p. 62.
[60] Morrison, *Beloved*, p. 64.
[61] Otten, p. 84.

with the tombstone marked, "Beloved," the characters in the story don't seem to recognize her or suspect her identity. When told her name, Paul D responds by saying: "Beloved. You use a last name, Beloved?"[62] Sethe even remembered the name as being the same as the one on the tombstone of her dead daughter, but she does not in the least bit suspect it to be the ghost which had haunted her all those years: "Sethe was particularly touched by her sweet name; the remembrance of glittering headstone made her feel especially kindly toward her."[63] The non-recognition of Beloved intensifies the element of the fantastic as the reader is left in a hesitation, a type of questioning limbo as to who she is. Why does she have the same name as the dead girl baby of the tomb? But she is a grown up woman? Is it possible that this woman could by some fantastic measure be the dead girl of the tomb?

Indeed, Beloved is the primary agent to deliver the fantastic in Morrison's novel. The element of the fantastic in *Beloved* has a function similar to that found in the genre element of horror; namely, fantasy is meant to preserve past memories important to the African-American community and present identity of the individuals of the community. In other words, the fantastic in Beloved

---

[62] Morrison, *Beloved*, p. 62.
[63] Morrison, *Beloved*, p. 63.

contributes to the scripturalizing *Tendenz* in *Beloved*. As it was in the case of the genre element of horror, the most important factor in the African-American past that fantasy seeks to preserve is the experience of slavery. The fantastic person of Beloved certainly serves to give slavery a resonance and an embodied presence [64] in the novel. Otten writes: "Beloved, then, is Sethe's doomed infant and one of the 'Sixty Million and More,' a victim both of Sethe's 'rough love' and the manifest cruelty of slavers."[65] And "Sixty Million and More" recalls to whom Morrison's novel is dedicated and refers to the number of blacks who were killed as captives in Africa or on slave ships and, therefore, never made it into slavery.[66] This correlation is significant and highlights the tragic experience of slavery; namely, the African participation in slavery.

Some black Africans often served as middlemen in the slave trade and, in effect, helped to institutionalize slavery. The violence done against Beloved by her own points towards the violence done against the

---

[64] Finney writes: "In *Beloved* Toni Morrison has personalized the legacy of slavery.... Ultimately the novel is as much concerned with the effects of that legacy on the Black community at large as the interaction between Sethe and Beloved" (Finney, p. 115).
[65] Otten, p. 84.
[66] Otten, p. 83.

enslaved Africans by their own. Beloved, therefore, functions to condemn the African participation in the creation of suffering. This is contextualized in the African-American context. When white slave owners came to claim Sethe, the runaway slave, who had been living in 124 Bluestone Road for a month, African-Americans in the neighborhood did not warn them. The narrative points out: "Not Ella, not John, not anybody ran down or to Bluestone Road, to say some new whitefolks with the Look just rode in. The righteous Look every Negro learned to recognize along with his ma'am's tit. Like a flag hoisted, this righteous telegraphed and announced the faggot, the whip, the fist, the lie, long before it went public."[67] The cause for not warning Sethe is attributed to "meanness."[68] If Sethe were warned in time as she should have been, she would not have panicked and Beloved probably would not have been killed. The narrative describes Sethe's panic:

> So Stamp Paid did not tell him how she flew, snatching up her children like a hawk on the wing; how her face beaked, how her hands worked like claws, how she collected them every which way:

---

[67] Morrison, *Beloved*, pp. 184-185.
[68] Morrison, *Beloved*, p. 185.

> one on her shoulder, one under her arm, one by the hand, the other shouted forward into the woodshed filled with just sunlight and shavings now because there wasn't any wood.

Thus, the blame is placed on the African-American community, which out of "meanness" did not help Sethe who was in need of their help. Harding and Martin concur: "At the same time, we discover that the fatal encounter is only made possible because the rest of the community spitefully abstains from giving the customary early-warning signal that would have given Sethe a chance to escape."[69] Little help could have prevented a great tragedy. Thus, Beloved embodies what went wrong in the African-American community.

Even though the African-American community contributed to the tragic result of the killing of Sethe's daughter by refusing to warn Sethe, they avoided Sethe and her house like a plague as if the fault was all hers. Beloved, therefore, embodies the resident evils of slavery that seem to drive African-American community asunder and debilitate those in the community who need the greatest help. Harding and Martin write:

---

[69] Harding and Martin, p. 138.

> In *Beloved*, Morrison once again considers the divisions threatening individual and community, but within a setting where they are both hyperdefined and in urgent need of reconciliation. The novel's community had survived the mutilating separations imposed under the brutal institution of slavery, and in the course of the novel they confront the aftermath of this institutionalized oppression. Among the freed blacks of post-Civil War Cincinnati, the most immediate divisions are the ones instigated from within the community. The women of 124 Bluestone Road lead a separate existence from the rest of the black community.[70]

Even after the slavery has ended officially, the evils of slavery linger on. Beloved's lingering on in Sethe's house is a fantastic representation of the experience of African-Americans. Beloved is a type of communal mirror.[71]

---

[70] Harding and Martin, p. 78.
[71] Caroline Rody writes: "In the dialectic between the lost past and the rememorying function of

Indeed, Beloved causes the characters in the novel to view themselves again and again and remember the past. Beloved as an element of fantasy has a functional purpose. Beloved's resident presence eventually ends up with her persecution of Sethe. It is a reminder that the vestiges of brutality and savagery of slavery could be passed on. The community needs to be united to fight Beloved, who actually represents slavery and its effects represented in the fantastic. Harding and Martin write:

> Beloved is not only the wrongful soul returned, but also, in a large mythic context, the emblem of all the suffering endured by the black people. She represents all forms of motherly desertions, the one imposed by the white slave dealers during the Middle passage as well as the original desertion of the African motherland.[72]

---

narrative love, *Beloved* reconceives the historical text as a transformative space: a space in which the present takes the past in a transforming embrace, constructed for mutual healing" (Caroline Rody, *The Daughter's Return: African-American and Caribbean Women's Fictions of History* (New York: Oxford University Press, 2001>, p. 29).

[72] Harding and Martin, p. 143.

In opposing Beloved, the African-American community confronted slavery and its memory. In standing with Sethe by their opposition of Beloved, the African-American community worked toward atoning for their passive participating in allowing ill-effects of slavery to continue. It is in the unification of the African-American community that Sethe finds redemption and Beloved, the emblematic reality of slavery and its ill-effects, is driven out.

Thus, Morrison effectively uses the genre element of fantasy in the character of Beloved to create a fantastic experience and an opportunity for reliving the past. Furthermore, the fantasy of Beloved allows for the characters to rectify past wrongs. The reader is implicitly encouraged to participate in the fantastic journey toward redemption.

As such, the fantastic element in *Beloved* is scripturalizing. It encourages remembrance of the past and a special identity for the future. The past, obviously, is the horrors of slavery. And the future identity is a communal togetherness whereby each help the other for individual and communal well-being. [73] This redemption may involve

---

[73] It is important to understand that African-American novelists experienced much difficulty in the twentieth century getting their works published (Major, p. 24). Given this experience of African-American novelists, it is not difficult to understand how community's moral obligation to help each other became such an important value. In this regard, it is relevant to note

ignoring or setting aside what would be deemed as immoral by dominant morality. Morrison, in fact, calls for moral standards to be placed on a different level – in recognition of the horrors of slavery. This is the primary function of the fantastic element of the character of Beloved and the fantastic experiences she creates in the novel. Likewise, the genre elements of horror, emphasizing the horrors of slavery work towards the same end.

Thus, Morrison effectively uses genre elements of horror and fantasy to achieve a type of African-American scripture in her work, *Beloved*. Harding and Martin write: "As a novelist Morrison is less interested in representing the Afro-American community naturalistically than she is in relaying myths and rituals that will enhance that community's cohesion in an era of discord and fragmentation."[74] Indeed, it is the collective dimension and communal and individual redemption from slavery and effects of slavery that Morrison tackles in her scripturalizing. Grewal writes that Morrison seeks "to make sense of the individual psyche and memory in wider social and

---

that African-American publishers often suffered along with African-American writers. Major writes: "All seem to share a common set of misfortunes: a lack of money and of trade support" (Major, p. 31).
[74] Harding and Martin, p. 112.

political terms."[75] And Morrison's scripturalizing is necessarily set against the background of domination. Otten explains:

> Her novels similarly reflect an amalgamation of mythic matter, depicting a world couched at times in seemingly contradictory truth: rebels becoming heroes, good creating evil; gardens that oppress, sins that redeem. They preserve the essential truth of myth by ironically modifying or reversing more orthodox assumptions of meaning.[76]

Indeed, Morrison's use of genre elements of horror and fantasy was intentional for creating a type of African-American scripture. *Beloved* represents her *magnum opus* which remembers/reminds the African-American experience of slavery and its horrible effects and encourages a redemptive participation in group identity and a new regenerative morality. *Beloved* is certainly an African-American scripture *par excellence*.

---

[75] Grewal, p. 14.
[76] Otten, p. 3.

Bibliography

Grewal, Gurleen. *Circles of Sorrow, Lines of Struggle*. Baton Rouge: Louisiana State University Press, 1998.

Gross, Seymour L., and John Edward Hardy (Ed.). *Images of the Negro in American Literature*. Chicago: The University of Chicago Press, 1966.

Harding, Wendy, and Jacky Martin. *A World of Difference: An Inter-Cultural Study of Toni Morrison's Novels*. Westport: Greenwood Press, 1994.

Huet, Marie Hélène. *Monstrous Imagination*. Cambridge: Harvard University Press, 1993.

Jackson, Rosemary. *Fantasy, the Literature of Subversion*. London: Methuen, 1981.

Major, Clarence. *The Dark and Feeling: Black American Writers and Their Work*. New York: The Third Press, 1974.

Mays, Benjamin E. *The Negro's God as Reflected in His Literature.* New York: Russell & Russell, 1938.

Morrison, Toni. "Behind the Making of *The Black Book.*" Black World 23 (February, 1974), pp. 86-90.

Morrison, Toni. *Beloved: A Novel.* New York: Vintage Books, 2004.

Morrison, Toni. "Rootedness: The Ancestor as Foundation" in *Black Women Writers (1950-1980): A Critical Evaluation.* Edited by Mari Evans. Garden City: Anchor Press/Doubleday, 1984.

Petesch, Donald A. *A Spy in the Enemy's Country: The Emergence of Modern Black Literature.* Iowa City: University of Iowa Press, 1989.

Oppenheimer, Paul. *Evil and the Demonic: A New Theory of Monstrous Behavior.* New York: New York University Press, 1996.

Otten, Terry. *The Crime of Innocence in the Fiction of Toni Morrison.* Columbia: University of Missouri Press, 1989.

Phillips, Kendall R. *Projected Fears: Horror Films and American Culture*. Westport: Praeger Publishers, 2005.

Rody, Caroline. *The Daughter's Return: African-American and Caribbean Women's Fictions of History*. New York: Oxford University Press, 2001.

Smith, Valerie. *Self-Discovery and Authority in Afro-American Narrative*. Cambridge: Harvard University Press, 1987.

Solomon, Barbara H. (Ed.). *Critical Essays on Toni Morrison's Beloved*. New York: G. K. Hall & Co., 1998.

Thomas, H. Nigel. *From Folklore to Fiction: A Study of Folk Heroes and Rituals in the Black American Novel*. New York: Greenwood Press, 1988.

Todorov, Tzvetan. *The Fantastic: A Structural Approach to a Literary Genre*. Translated by Richard Howard. Ithaca: Cornell University Press, 1975.

Justin Martyr and his Biblical Epistemology[1]

Many studies have been done on the influence of Platonic thought on Justin Martyr. After all, Justin Martyr was the first Christian thinker to use lovgo" spermatikov" to describe relationship between God and humans. Other Greek philosophical terms and concepts flavor his writings. But to accuse Justin of total dependence, or even a significant dependence, on Greek philosophy would be a grave mistake. Such presupposition would only serve as a microscope and, thereby, hinder the historian from grasping the overall picture of the person and thought of Justin Martyr.

Justin Martyr converted to Christianity after a long journey through different philosophical schools. Justin believed that he had found true philosophy in Christianity and claimed that the Old Testament and the Gospels served as proof. Wearing a philosopher's cloak, Justin Martyr employed biblical epistemology and typology in his defense of Christianity. In the process of his

---

[1] I would like to thank Professor Ronald Mellor for reading the paper and commenting on it in 1993. Then, Professor Mellor was the chairman of the History Department at UCLA.

apologetic, Justin Martyr laid a foundation for Christian theology, particularly in the theology of the Trinity and Christology. One sees Justin's biblical epistemology and apologetic in the *First Apology*, which served as a foundation for his other writings, including *Dialogue with Trypho the Jew* and *Second Apology*.[2]

---

[2]Justin wrote his First Apology in 151 AD, after he moved from Ephesus to Rome. Although Justin held a dialogue with Trypho in 135 AD, soon after his conversion to Christianity, Justin wrote the Dialogue with Trypho the Jew about 160 AD (Henry Chadwick, The Early Church (London: Penguin Books, 1967), 75). Thus, Justin's oral apologies were formalized in the First Apology. This written apology provided structure to his later writings and also to his written depiction of his conversation with Trypho some twenty-five years ago. Eric Osborn agrees with Chadwick's account (Justin Martyr (Tübingen: J. C. B. Mohr (Paul Siebeck), 1973), 8), as does the majority of the scholars on the period. But Erwin Goodenough disagrees. He speculates that Justin's discussion with Trypho did not occur, but that Dialogue with Trypho was "the monologue of a victor" (The Theology of Justin Martyr (Amsterdam: Philo Press, 1968), 40). This is in keeping with Goodenough's other speculative assertions in his book. For example, he also argues that Justin's journey through different philosophical schools was Justin's fabrication as was his conversation with the old man which brought Justin to conversion (58). Goodenough does not have any historical proof to support his assertions, except speculative literary criticism. Goodenough's discussion of Greek philosophy contributes to the understanding of the relationship

Different elements of Justin's writings compelled scholars to suspect a severe Greek influence. Even the title of Justin's first written work, *First Apology*, is reminiscent of an another work: Plato's *Apology of Socrates*. Thus, it is no surprise to find Justin depicting Socrates as a martyr for the truth. Justin writes:

> When Socrates tried by true reason and with due inquiry to make these things clear and to draw men away from the demons, they, working through men who delighted in wickedness, managed to have him put to death as godless and impious, saying that he was bringing in new divinities. And now they do the same kind of thing to us.[3]

Justin, therefore, places persecuted Christians on the same level as Socrates and his apology in the same class as that of Socrates. Cyril Richardson assumes that Jus-

---

between Justin and Greek philosophy, but his speculations on Justin's life are not dependable.

[3]First Apology, 5.12-17. All quotes of the First Apology are from the translation of Cyril C. Richardson, found in pages 242-289 of his book, Early Christian Fathers (New York: Collier Books, 1970).

tin's use of the classical literary form of apology was intentional:

> The first Christian writers, indeed, clearly had classical literary forms in mind, since they wrote in some hope of reaching a general audience. An apology is by definition a speech for the defense. The use of the form for philosophic propaganda goes back to the illustrious example of Plato's Apology of Socrates. It is this surely that brings Socrates so naturally to Justin's mind in the First Apology....[4]

---

[4] 226. Richardson argues that the First Apology functioned more as "a manual for inquirers," depicting faith and practice of Christians of the second century, rather than as a defensive document (228). Hans von Campenhausen agrees with Richardson that Justin wrote for everyone who would read. But Campenhausen considers the First Apology as "the most impressive evidence" of Justin's evangelical intentions and not merely as a manual on Christian faith and practice. For Campenhausen, Justin wrote to convert his readers to Christianity (The Fathers of the Greek Church, tr. Stanley Godman (New York: Pantheon, 1959), 18). Goodenough agrees with Richardson and Campenhausen that Justin wrote for a general audience but disagrees that the letter was ever intended for Emperor Antoninus Pius. Justin addressed the letter to the emperor only to give it public

dignity (Goodenough 82). Goodenough's claim that the letter was never intended for the emperor is misguided speculation. Goodenough bases his claims on the thesis that Justin's apologetic letter was dependent on the apologetic tradition of Hellenistic Judaism; thus, Goodenough draws parallels between Justin and Philo of Alexandria. Historical data confirms Goodenough's erroneous assumptions. First of all, book 28 of the Dialogue with Trypho shows that Justin was an uncircumcised gentile -- Justin was born a non-Jew and he stayed a non-Jew. Second of all, Justin was trained in Greek philosophy and converted to Christianity; there is no evidence of influences from Hellenistic Judaism or Philo. Actually, Justin's hermenuetic markedly differs from Philo's in that Justin utilizes typology, whereas Philo utilizes the allegorical method. Not only is it historically inaccurate to assert dependence of Justin on Hellenistic Judaism, it is further faulty to claim that Justin never intended the letter to reach Emperor Antoninus Pius. After all, Justin wore the philosopher's cloak and wrote the First Apology soon after his move from Ephesus to Rome. Furthermore, Roman persecution on Christians saw a decline in 151 AD, the date of the First Apology. Also, Justin found himself in the midst of the Second Sophistic movement. Mid-second century saw a renewed interest in philosophy, rhetoric, and medicine. Galen interested significant figures in the Roman empire, like Emperor Marcus Aurelius, as well as the general public, in medical lectures and handbooks on diseases. Therefore, the cult of Asclepius also experienced a renaissance. Thus, it is definitely conceivable in this period of much philosophical interest for Justin in his philosopher's cloak with pupils of his own to expect to gain an open ear from Emperor Antoninus Pius. (Information regarding the Second Sophistic movement is from G. W. Bowersock's Greek

Indeed, such contention seems congruent with other aspects of Justin's writings that seem to show a Greek influence.

Justin's use of *logos spermatikos* in *Second Apology* particularly seems to confirm accusations of Greek influence on Justin. Justin claims that Plato, Stoics, Greek poets and historians perceived partial truth due to their participation in *the logos spermatikos*:

> For each one of them, seeing, through his participation of the seminal Divine Word, what was related to it, spoke very well. .... Indeed, all writers, by means of the engrafted seed of the Word which was implanted in them, had a dim glimpse of the truth. For the seed of something and its imitation, given in proportion to one's capacity, is one thing, but the thing itself, which is shared and imitated according to His grace, is quite another.[5]

Sophists in the Roman Empire (Oxford: Clarendon Press, 1969)).
[5] Second Apology, 13.9-12; 19-24. All quotes of the Second Apology are from Thomas B. Falls' translation found in pages 119-135 of Writings of Saint Justin Martyr (New York: Christian Heritage, Inc., 1948).

Justin argues that these individuals suffered because of their participation in the *logos spermatikos*:

> We know that the followers of the Stoic teaching, because they were praiseworthy at least in their ethics, as were also the poets in some respects, because of the seed of reason implanted in all mankind, were hated and killed.[6]

Justin, however, distinguishes the participants of the seminal Word from the whole Word: "the whole Word, which is Christ."[7]

Several scholars, thus, point to Justin's use of *logos spermatikos* and claim Stoic influences. Goodenough, one such scholar, argues:

> ... the Stoics used the spermatic Logos for similes and metaphors of all kinds, and particularly in cosmological descriptions and in attempts at accommodating Greek myths. The term spermatic Logos was applied figuratively to God, for example, in

---

[6]Second Apology, 8.1-4.
[7]Second Apology, 8.13.

the passage of Diogenes Laertes VII.134-137.[8]

Goodenough argues further that Justin misunderstood and misused the term, *logos spermatikos*, since Justin equated it with his Incarnate Logos, Jesus Christ, whom he considered to be the same *ousia* of God the Father,[9] the Cosmic Principle. When Stoics used *logos spermatikos* in reference to divinity, they did so only figuratively. Not only that, Stoicism never lost its original denotation of *logos spermatikos*, which had

---

[8] 17.

[9] Justin argues for the divinity of Jesus Christ, the Incarnate Logos. This poses a problem for monotheistic Christianity. After all, Justin himself is concerned with emphasizing monotheism, as is clearly evident in his treatise, The Monarchy, in which Justin utilizes Greek literature to prove monotheism. Justin's emphasis of Jesus Christ as God seems to present two Gods -- God the Father and the Divine Logos, Jesus Christ. Trypho the Jew points this out in chapter 55 of the Dialogue with Trypho. Justin's answer to this problem is subordinationism; Justin states in book 13 of the First Apology that God is first, Jesus Christ is second, and the Holy Spirit is third "in rank." Thus, he maintains distinctiveness of the "persons" of the Trinity, while maintaining the same divine substance. His reaction against Marcion, who claimed the existence of different Gods for the Old Testament and the New Testament, most likely propelled him to a subordinationist position, which the Council of Nicea in 325 AD rectified to a doctrine of co-equal existence of the Trinity.

scientific implications. Goodenough states: "Loosely then, as the term spermatic Logos was later used, there seems no ground for believing that in strict Stoic thought the spermatic Logos ever lost its proper biological signification...."[10]

What was the original meaning of *logos spermatikos*? Goodenough describes: "*Logos spermatikos* was in Stoic physics a biological term to account for the persistence of types and groups from one generation to another."[11] The Stoics, being nominalists, denied the existence of types, such as "dog," which include in its class certain living forms with similar qualities; they preferred to recognize only individual dogs. But they were faced with a problem; not only did dogs beget dogs, individual dogs, such as spaniels, reproduced dogs with qualities pertaining to spaniels. Thus, the Stoics utilized *logos spermatikos* to describe survival of types and of individual characteristics in successive generations. The Stoics believed that every animal and plant had *pneuma* at the center of its being; for animals, this center is located in the heart. This *pneuma* flows out into a living being's whole body, and it is this "gaseous flow" that gives sight to the eyes, hearing to the ears, and the power of speech to the voice. In cohabitation, *pneuma* flows from both the

---

[10] 18.
[11] 16.

male and the female and contributes to the complete seed, which carries on the type and individual traits. The Stoics called this pneumatic element, *logos spermatikos*.[12]

As noted before, Goodenough argues that Justin Martyr shows dependence on Stoicism because he used the term, *logos spermatikos*, although he did not properly use it. Yet, how viable is this thesis? Justin Martyr did use the term; that is beyond dispute. But mere use of a term does not denote dependence. Goodenough agrees that Justin did not use the term in the way the Stoics normally used them, but he attributes this to Justin's inadequacy to grasp the concept.[13] For Goodenough, Justin had all the intentions of utilizing Greek philosophy.

Such reasoning of Goodenough is a good example of *a priori* argumentation. It is easy for a scholar to argue from the vantage point of his presumption. Goodenough falls into this trap. He wants to prove Justin's dependence on Greek philosophy, so

---

[12]Goodenough 16-17.
[13] Goodenough asserts that Justin's account of his philosophical training is a fabrication. Goodenough speculates: "...the chances are very probable that Justin's adventures in the philosophical schools are as ideal as his conversation with the old man which introduced him to Christianity" (58). Goodenough's use of words, such as "chances" and "probable," point to Goodenough's uncertainty. Indeed, there is no historical evidence that supports Goodenough's speculation concerning Justin's philosophical training.

he speculates to reach his conclusion. But Justin's use of terms normally associated with Greek philosophy does not prove Justin's dependence on Greek philosophy and thought.

It is clear from Justin Martyr's writings that he was not interested in utilizing Greek philosophy. To be an effective apologist, Justin utilized terms found in Greek philosophy and understood by his audience; after all, Justin's purpose was to sway his audience to his viewpoint and to the Christian faith.

Indeed, a broader examination of Justin's writings shows that Justin used biblical epistemology and typology as a basis of his apologetic. Even Justin's Logos theology is more dependent on the prologue of the Gospel of John than on Greek philosophy.

To understand Justin's biblical epistemology, one needs to examine Justin's "truth," which forms the core of his epistemology. After all, Justin's *First Apology* appeals to the philosopher's love of truth: "Reason requires that those who are truly pious and philosophers should honor and cherish the truth alone, scorning merely to follow the opinions of the ancients, if they are worthless."[14] For Justin, true philosophers pursue truth. Not only that, true philosophers act according to the truth, even

---

[14] 2.1-4.

if it brings them death. Justin writes: "... the lover of truth ought to choose in every way, even at the cost of his own life, to speak and do what is right, though death should take him away."[15] Thus, Justin appeals his apologetic to Emperor Antoninus Pius the philosopher, a lover of the truth: "So do you, since you are called pious and philosophers and guardians of justice and lovers of culture, at least give us a hearing -- and it will appear if you are really such."[16]

But Justin's truth was not an abstract idea; for Justin, the Christian scriptures, particularly the Old Testament and the Gospels, were the only truths. Justin writes:

> In order to make this clear to you I will present the evidence that the things we say, as disciples of Christ and the prophets who came before him, are the only truths and older than all the writers who have lived, and we ask to be accepted, not because we say the same things as they do, but because we are speaking the truth....[17]

---

[15] First Apology, 2.5-8.
[16] First Apology, 2.8-10.
[17] First Apology, 23.1-6.

Because Justin believed that the scriptures were the truth, he exuded confidence even against renown Greek thinkers. Justin believed that Plato sat at the feet of Moses. Moses' thoughts made imprints on the ideas of Plato, as well as on those of other Greek thinker, because Moses preceded Plato and Greek thinkers. Justin writes:

> So when Plato said, "The blame belongs to him who chooses, and God is free from blame," he took this from the prophet Moses. For Moses was earlier than Plato and all the Greek writers. And everything that philosophers and poets said about the immortality of the soul, punishments after death, contemplation of heavenly things, and teachings of that kind -- they took hints from the prophets and so were able to understand these things and expound them.[18]

All truths found in Greek thinkers were, in essence, from the Old Testament.

But one does not find the whole truth among Greek thinkers, because evil

---

[18] First Apology, 44.22-29.

demons[19] effectively deceived them. Justin writes:

> But those who hand on the myths invented by the poets offer no demonstration to the youngsters who learn them -- indeed I [am prepared to] show that they were told at the instigation of the wicked demons to deceive and lead astray the human race.[20]

Just as the evil demons embodied in the form of a Serpent[21] in the Garden of Eden persuaded and led Adam and Eve away from God, the holder of all truth, by means of lies,

---

[19] Justin shows greater interest in demons than his contemporaries. In later Platonism and popular Greek thought, "demon" was a morally neutral term, ascribed to intermediate beings. That explains why Justin usually used a negative qualifier before the word, "demon" or "demons" (Richardson 233-234).
[20] First Apology, 54.1-5.
[21] "Serpent" is one of the titles that Justin favors using for "evil demons." Justin writes: "Among us the chief of the evil demons is called the serpent and Satan and the devil, as you can learn by examining our writings" (First Apology, 28.1-3). The "serpent" is a clear reference to the Genesis story's tempter who led Eve to eat of the fruit of the Tree of the Knowledge of Good and Evil, which God had forbidden. For Justin, this title is most appropos, because evil demons distort the truth in order to lead people away from the truth.

evil demons effectively led many humans astray by causing poets to misunderstand prophecies regarding Jesus Christ and to write myths that misled people. For example, when people heard a prophecy concerning Jesus Christ found in the Old Testament, such as "Strong as a giant to run his course,"[22] they misunderstood this to be applicable to Heracles, who, the Greek poets claimed, was strong and traveled over the whole earth. Also, when people heard prophecies about how Jesus Christ would heal every disease and raise the dead, they pointed to Asclepius. Thus, people either pointed to Greek gods and worshiped their image, or dismissed those prophecies about the person and work of Jesus Christ with the contention that what was said about Jesus Christ was no different from what was said about mythic gods -- they were fictional literature.[23] Thus, evil demons used Greek thinkers to distort the truth and deceive people.

Justin believed that the whole truth could be found only in the holy scriptures. Why did Justin Martyr consider the Old Testament and the Gospels as truths? For Justin, the Old Testament foretold what would happen, especially about Jesus Christ, and the Gospel accounts confirmed the

---

[22] Justin is quoting from Psalm 19:5b.
[23] First Apology, 54.5ff.

fulfilment of the Old Testament. Justin writes:

> We do not trust in mere hearsay, but are forced to believe those who prophesied [these things] before they happened, because we actually see things that have happened and are happening as was predicted. This will, as we think, be the greatest and surest demonstration to you too.[24]

Justin, thereupon, explains how biblical prophecies were fulfilled. Justin provides a passage from Moses and explains that the passage was prophetic of Jesus Christ and found fulfillment in him. Justin writes:

> Thus, Moses, who was the first of the prophets, said in these very words: "The ruler shall not depart from Judah, nor the governor from his thighs, until he come for whom it is reserved; and he shall be the expectation of the nations, binding his colt to the vine, washing his robe in

---

[24] First Apology, 30.5-10.

the blood of the grape."[25] You can inquire precisely and learn up to whose time the Jews had their own ruler and king. [It was] until the manifesttation of Jesus Christ, our teacher and the expounder of the unrecognized prophecies, as was predicted by the divine and holy prophetic Spirit through Moses, that a ruler would not depart from the Jews until he should come for whom the Kingdom is reserved.[26]

Justin continues on to explain that Moses' prophecy, "binding his colt to the vine," refers to Jesus' triumphal entry into Jerusalem on, what we now refer to as, the Palm Sunday. Soon afterwards, he was crucified, thereby "washing his robe in the blood of the grape."[27] Thus, Justin believed that the scriptures were the truth because prophecy found fulfillment in Jesus Christ.

Although the passage from Genesis, quoted within Justin's text above and attributed to Moses, corresponds to the

---

[25]Justin is quoting from Genesis 49:10-11.
[26]First Apology, 32.1-12.
[27]First Apology, 32.21ff.

actual biblical text,[28] Justin was not always faithful in his scriptural quotations. But Justin's argument was consistent; Justin contended that the scriptures were truth because they were fulfilled. Justin writes:

> Isaiah, another prophet, prophesying the same things in other words, said: "A star shall rise out of Jacob, and a flower will come forth from the root of Jesse, and upon his arm will the nations hope." The shining star has risen and the flower has grown from the root of Jesse -- this is Christ.[29]

It is clear that Justin is interested in establishing the fulfillment of prophecy in Christ Jesus.

A closer textual examination shows that the reference, attributed to Isaiah, comes

---

[28] Genesis 49:10-11 is provided for the sake of comparison: "The scepter will not depart from Judah, nor the ruler's staff from between his feet, until he comes to whom it belongs and the obedience of the nations is his. He will tether his donkey to a vine, his colt to the choicest branch; he will wash his garments in wine, his robe in the blood of grapes" (NIV). One should note that even this scriptural passage has some differences with Justin's reference provided in book 32 of his First Apology.
[29] First Apology, 32.41-46.

from two distinct places in the book of Isaiah -- Isaiah 11:1 and Isaiah 51:5. Isaiah 11:1 reads: "A shoot will come from the stump of Jesse; from his roots a Branch will bear fruit" (NIV). The part of Justin's reference, "a flower will come forth from the root of Jesse," finds its parallel in Isaiah 11:1a: "A shoot will come from the stump of Jesse."

And Isaiah 51:5 reads: "My righteousness draws near speedily, my salvation is on the way, and my arm will bring justice to the nations. The islands will look for me and wait in hope for my arms" (NIV). The part of Justin's reference, "upon his arm will the nations hope," finds its counterpart in Isaiah 51:5b: "The islands will look for me and wait in hope for my arms."

Not only that, a part of Justin's reference to "Isaiah" finds its scriptural place in Numbers 24:17. Numbers 24:17 reads: "I see him, but not now; I behold him, but not near. A star will come out of Jacob; a scepter will rise out of Israel. He will crush the foreheads of Moab, the skulls of all the sons of Sheth" (NIV). There is an obvious correlation between the part of Justin's reference, "A star shall rise out of Jacob," and Numbers 24:17b: "A star will come out of Jacob...."

It is clear that Justin synthesizes three distinct biblical references into one quote, and he attributes the synthesized quote to Isaiah, although a part of it is from Numbers.[30] But this is congruent with his understanding of the truth and his biblical epistemology.

Justin believed that the holy scriptures were the truth, not because prophets spoke it, but because the Word revealed it to the prophets. It was the involvement of the divine Logos that made the prophecies whole truth, and not partial truth. It was, therefore, the prophecy of the divine Logos that found fulfillment. In essence, the whole Old Testament found its author in the Logos, and the prophets were mere instruments. Justin writes: "When you hear the words of the prophets spoken as in a particular character, do not think of them as spoken by the inspired men themselves, but by the divine Word that moved them."[31] Thus, the Old

---

[30] Such synthesized quotation finds precedence in the Gospels. For example, in his Gospel, Mark presents a passage, which he attributes to "Isaiah," as a prophecy concerning John the Baptizer. Gospel of Mark 1:2-4 reads: "It is written in Isaiah the prophet: 'I will send my messenger ahead of you, who will prepare your way' -- 'a voice of one calling in the desert, "Prepare the way for the Lord, make straight paths for him."' And so John came, baptizing in the desert region and preaching a baptism of repentance for the forgiveness of sins" (NIV). When examined closely, one finds that the passage attributed to Isaiah is from two separate sources -- Malachi 3:1, which composes the first part of Mark's quote of "Isaiah," and Isaiah 40:3, which parallels the second part.
[31] First Apology, 36.1-4.

Testament is a recording of the prophecies of the Logos.

But there were those who misunderstood the Old Testament prophecies, according to Justin. For even if one has the Old Testament in one's hand, as the Jews did as well as the Egyptians, one cannot understand, unless one is given understanding. In *First Apology*, Justin describes the addition of the Septuagint to the Egyptian library in Alexandria. Justin accounts:

> When Ptolemy, king of Egypt, was founding a library, and set out to gather the writings of all mankind, he learned about these prophecies and sent to Herod, then king of the Jews, asking him to send him the prophetic books. King Herod sent them, written in the aforementioned Hebrew language. Since their contents were not intelligible to the Egyptians, he again sent and asked him to send men who could translate them into Greek. This was done, and the books remain in the hands of the Egyptians down to the pre-

sent; the Jews everywhere have them too.[32]

Thus, the translation of the Old Testament into Greek increased readership. But even with the Old Testament, non-Christians did not understand the truth provided by the Old Testament prophecies. Justin argues that it is this inability to understand the Old Testament prophecies that induced some non-Christians to persecute the Christians. Justin states: "But though they read them, they do not understand what they say, but consider us their enemies and opponents, putting us to death or punishing us, as you do ...."[33] So it was possible to possess the written truth of the divine Logos, namely the Old Testament, and still not comprehend the whole truth.

Justin, therefore, emphasized that it is the divine Logos that reveals all truths. One knows the truth because the truth is made known to him by the divine Logos through sundry means. Justin writes concerning the work of the divine Logos: "For sometimes he speaks as predicting the things that are to happen, sometimes he speaks as in the character of God the Master of all, sometimes as in the character of Christ, sometimes in the character of people an-

---

[32]First Apology, 31.6-16.
[33]First Apology, 31.16-19.

swering the Lord or his Father."[34] Justin believes that the divine Logos is the only source of whole truth.

Using such epistemology, Justin Martyr encourages one to ask God[35] for the knowledge of the truth. Justin writes: "Above all, beseech God to open to you the gates of light, for no one can perceive or understand these truths unless he has been enlightened by God and His Christ."[36] For Justin, God holds the truth, so only God and Jesus Christ, who is also God in Justin's mind, can reveal the truth.

And since the holy scriptures are a written revelation of God's truth for Justin, Justin uses them profusely in his apologetic. Indeed, Justin's works testify to his biblical epistemology; one knows what one knows by the economy of the Logos. And since the divine Logos revealed the whole truth in the holy scriptures, one knows that one knows only through the scriptures. The holy scriptures confirm whether one knows the truth

---

[34] First Apology, 36.4-8.
[35] One needs to keep in mind that Justin considered the Logos as God in essence; thus, there was no real metaphysical distinction between God and the Logos. There was only one God.
[36] Dialogue with Trypho, 7.26-29. All quotes of the Dialogue with Trypho are from Thomas B. Falls' translation found in pages 147-366 of Writings of Saint Justin Martyr (New York: Christian Heritage, Inc., 1948).

or not. Francis Osborn comments regarding Justin's sentiments on the holy scriptures:

> Justin speaks of the climax of his search for truth as reading the words of the prophets and the words of the saviour, and finding there the only sound and useful philosophy. The scriptures answer the questions which philosophy has asked, concerning the beginning and end of things. The scriptures present a coherent statement of doctrine in important matters and this coherence makes them the philosophy par excellence.[37]

Justin believed that the scriptures present the best philosophy, since they are the truth and answer important questions in life. Justin's regard for the holy scriptures is not surprising in light of his conversion story.

Justin did not come from a Christian family. His conversion to Christianity came after he traveled through different philosophical schools in search of truth. Justin describes his own journey through different philosophical schools in chapter two of his *Dialogue with Trypho*. When Justin first became interested in philosophical inquiry,

---

[37]99.

Justin made himself a student of a Stoic, but Justin left his Stoic teacher because he believed that the Stoic had no knowledge of God and no interest in such a knowledge. Justin, then, placed himself under the tutelage of a Peripatetic. But when the Peripatetic teacher demanded a fee that would profit him, Justin considered him to be not a real philosopher and left him. Because Justin still was yearning for philosophical knowledge, he turned to another philosopher, "a very famous Pythagorean." When Justin expressed his desire to be his student, the Pythagorean teacher asked Justin if he knew music, astronomy, and geometry. The Pythagorean teacher expounded on the necessity of expertise in these studies for a proper philosophical inquiry. But when Justin admitted to a lack of knowledge of these fields, the Pythagorean dismissed him. With a troubled state of mind, Justin turned to the Platonists and found satisfaction in Platonism. Justin tells Trypho:

> The perception of incorporeal things quite overwhelmed me and the Platonic theory of ideas added wings to my mind, so that in a short time I imagined myself a wise man. So great was my folly that I fully expected immediately to

gaze upon God, for this is the
goal of Plato's philosophy.[38]

In such state of mind, Justin met the old man who led him to conversion.

Justin was walking toward his favorite place of thinking with the intention of being alone, but an old man was following him. Justin gave a sharp stare at the old man, and that started the conversation that eventually led to Justin's conversion. At first, Justin and the old man discussed different topics in philosophy, such as, whether philosophy produces happiness. Justin stated that it does, because it gives knowledge of those things that exist. The old man led this epistemological discussion to a theological level, such as the inquiry of the nature of God. Justin argued that the soul could see God through the intellect, even when it is in the body, but it is not a clear sight. The soul beholds God clearly, when it is released from the body. Then the old man asked Justin, if the soul, which had perceived God clearly in its separate state, would remember what it beheld when again joined to the body. Justin replied in the negative. Then, the old man asked a practical question. What is the advantage of having seen God if one cannot remember it? Justin did not know how to respond to this. At this juncture, the old man argued that the philoso-

---

[38]Dialogue with Trypho, 2.55-60.

phers, who cannot even explain the nature of the soul, know nothing. Justin, thereupon, asked for a method or a teacher that he should follow. Then the old man told Justin about the prophets of the Old Testament, who reiterated what they saw and heard from the inspiration of the Holy Spirit. The old man told Justin that these prophecies were fulfilled and were being fulfilled. After Justin heard the old man's argument that knowledge and truth are found in Christianity, Justin converted.[39] Justin comments about his conversion experience:

> But my spirit was immediately set on fire, and an affection for the prophets, and for those who are friends of Christ, took hold of me; while pondering on his words, I discovered that his was the only sure and useful philosophy. Thus it is that I am now a philosopher.[40]

Justin, thus, believed that he had found answers to his philosophical questions in Christianity. For Justin, that which provided truth and knowledge was the true philosophy. And the divine Logos, or Jesus Christ, was the source of the whole truth. The

---

[39] Dialogue with Trypho, 3-8.
[40] Dialogue with Trypho, 8.4-8.

divine Logos inspired the Old Testament prophet to reveal the truth, the most important of which was concerning the person and work of Jesus Christ.

The divine Logos provided the whole truth and inspired prophets to tell of this truth; Greek philosophers only had partial truth. And among the Greek thinkers, there were those whom the evil demons used to distort the truth and lead people away from the whole truth of the divine Logos. In light of this information and, more importantly, in light of Justin's biblical epistemology and typology, it would be misleading to say that Greek philosophy had a great influence on Justin Martyr and his thought. His thoughts were motivated by his truth, which, he believed, was contained in the Old Testament and the Gospels.

Justin's dependence on the scriptures is evident in Justin's description of the Logos. One can see that Justin's Logos philosophy and theology were more dependent on the prologue of the Gospel of John. One sees from the Gospel of John that the author [41] presents the Logos as God in

---

[41] The authorship of the Gospel of John is debated. In Against Heresies, written about 180 AD, Irenaeus provides the traditional view that the author was John the son of Zebedee, who wrote the gospel at an old age. But even in the second half of the second century, anti-Montanists attributed the gospel to the Gnostic Cerinthus. Werner Kümmel, in his widely accepted Introduction to the New Testament, argues

essence, but also as a separate hypostasis.[42] Gospel of John 1:1-2 reads: "In the beginning was the Word, and the Word was with God, and the Word was God. He was with God in the beginning" (NIV). It is clear here that the author believes both in the unity and the separate quality of the Logos and God. This Logos was intricately involved in the creation of the world: "Through him all things were made; without him nothing was made that has been made" (John 1:3 NIV). This divine Logos became incarnate in Jesus Christ, according to the author of the Gospel of John: "The Word became flesh and made his dwelling among us. We have seen his glory, the glory of the One and Only, who came from the Father, full of grace and truth" (1:14 NIV).

---

against both positions and claims that it is impossible to clearly ascertain the author. But Kümmel states that John the son of Zebedee is definitely not the author because Jesus' discourses in the gospel show influences from Gnostic language, thereby making it impossible for an eyewitness of Jesus to be the author (tr. Howard Kee (Nashville: Abingdon Press, 1975), 239-246).

[42] Although "hypostasis" is a word that comes from the trinitarian debates of the fourth century, its usage here is appropos, since the Gospel of John's Logos theology and Justin's thoughts regarding distinct numbers in the Godhead contributed greatly to the trinitarian theology and its language of speaking of the numbers of the Trinity as "hypostasis," or "persona."

And it is only this Logos who reveals the truth; the divine Logos alone, therefore, functions as the source of truth. Gospel of John 1:18 reads: "No one has ever seen God, but God the One and Only,[43] who is at the Father's side, has made him known" (NIV). But not all people accepted this Logos, including the Jews, his own people: "He was in the world, and though the world was made through him, the world did not recognize him. He came to that which was his own, but his own did not receive him" (John 1:10-11 NIV).

These ideas found in the prologue of the Gospel of John clearly parallel Justin Martyr's thoughts. Justin believed that the divine Logos was, in essence, God, but distinct in number. This is clearly seen in Justin's assertion to Trypho that the Logos was involved in the creation process. Because there is more than one number in the Godhead, God uses a plural first person pronoun in the Genesis account of the creation. Justin describes his discussion with Trypho:

> 'My friends,' I continued, 'the word of God, through Moses, stated exactly the same thing, when it revealed to us that at the creation of man God

---

[43]"God the One and Only" is a reference to the divine Logos (cf. John 1:14).

spoke of Him [the divine Logos] (who was pointed out by Moses) in the same sense. Here is the Scriptural passage: "Let us make man to Our image and likeness ...."[44] .... These are the word of Moses "And God said: Behold Adam is become as one of Us, knowing good and evil."[45] Now, the words "as one of Us" clearly show that there were a number of persons together, and they were at least two. .... But this Offspring, who was truly begotten of the Father talked with Him before all creation ....'[46]

Justin, therefore, emphasizes that there are more than one person in the Godhead. For Justin, the divine Logos is God in essence and separate from God in number. This divine Logos actively participated in the creation process. The analogy with the prologue to the Gospel of John is obvious.

Furthermore, there is an analogy between revelatory aspects of the Logos in the prologue to the Gospel of John and in the writings of Justin Martyr. Just as the

---

[44] Justin is quoting from Genesis 1:26a.
[45] Justin is quoting from Genesis 3:22a.
[46] Dialogue with Trypho, 62.1-5, 21-25, 29-31.

author of the Gospel of John claims that the knowledge of God was made known by the Logos, Justin claims that the Logos is the source of the whole truth, as noted above. Also, the author of the prologue and Justin are in agreement with regard to people's rejection of the truth. The author of the prologue asserts that people did not recognize the Logos and "his own," namely the Jews, did not accept him. This parallels Justin Martyr's argument mentioned above that, although Jews and other non-Christians had access to the Old Testament prophecies, they misunderstood the truths in them and sought to persecute Christians, rather than join them in accepting the Logos Incarnate, Jesus Christ.

Such parallels inspired Cyril Richardson to comment: "His writings have the additional interest of being the most specifically Christian of the ancient Apologies."[47] Indeed, the prologue of the Gospel of John shows much influence on Justin's thoughts.

It is clear that Justin Martyr based his arguments on the holy scriptures. After all, Justin considered the scriptures as written truths, which the Logos presented to the humankind through inspired prophets. The scriptures alone held the key to the knowledge of the truth; this was clear from the fact that the prophecies of the Old

---

[47] 228.

Testaments were fulfilled, especially in Jesus Christ, and were continuously being fulfilled.

Although a superficial glance might persuade one to quickly announce the judgment of strong Greek influence on Justin, a closer examination compels one to conclude that Justin utilized similar language as the Greek thinkers but only in order to forward his truths that he found in the holy scriptures. Thus, using biblical epistemology, Justin exerted great influence on behalf of Christianity as well as on Christianity.[48]

---

[48] Scholars have much praise for Justin Martyr. Henry Chadwick comments: "Justin Martyr occupies a central position in the history of Christian thought of the second century" (79). Cyril Richardson states: "Justin Martyr is one of the greatest of the Apologists" (228). Francis Osborn gives a greater praise: "Justin is the greatest of the apologists" (13). Hans von Campenhausen gives the greatest praise: "It is wrong to place him alongside the other apologists as if he were merely part of a larger group and typical of a general intellectual current. The later champions of Christianity such as Tatian and Athenagoras nearly all learned from him, and he stands head and shoulders above the earlier ones like Aristides and the little known Quadratus" (13).

Bibliography

Bowersock, G. W. *Greek Sophists in the Roman Empire*. Oxford: Clarendon Press, 1969.

Chadwick, Henry. *The Early Church*. London: Penguin Books, 1967.

Eusebius. *The History of the Church from Christ to Constantine*. Tr. G. A. Williamson.. London: Penguin Books, 1965.

Farmer, David Hugh. *The Oxford Dictionary of Saints*. Oxford: Clarendon Press, 1978.

Farrar, Frederic W. *Lives of the Fathers*. Edinburgh: Adam and Charles Black, 1889.

Goodenough, Erwin R. *The Theology of Justin Martyr*. Amsterdam: Philo Press, 1968.

Hyldahl, Niels. *Philosophie und Christentum*. Kopenhagen: Prostant apud Munksgaard, 1966.

Justin Martyr. *Writings of Saint Justin Martyr*. Tr. Thomas B. Falls. New York: Christian Heritage, Inc., 1948.

Kaye, John. *The First Apology of Justin Martyr*. London: Griffith Farran Browne & Co. Ltd.

Kümmel, Werner G. *Introduction to the New Testament*. Tr. Howard C. Lee. Nashville: Abingdon Press, 1975.

Osborn, Eric Francis. *Justin Martyr*. Tübingen: J. C. B. Mohr (Paul Siebeck), 1973.

Prigent, Pierre. *Justin et l'Ancien Testament*. Paris: Librairie Lecoffre, 1964.

Richardson, Cyril C. (Tr. and Ed.) *Early Christian Fathers*. New York: Collier Books, 1970.

Stylianopoulos, Theodore. *Justin Martyr and the Mosaic Law*. Missoula: Scholars Press, 1975.

Von Campenhausen, Hans. *The Fathers of the Greek Church*. Tr. Stanley Godman. New York: Pantheon, 1959.

Justin Martyr and his Biblical Epistemology

The Holy Bible (New International Version). Grand Rapids: Zondervan Publishing House, 1989.

Historical Implications of Nestorius and Cyril's Theological Differences in the Fifth Century AD[1]

"Who do you say I am?"[2] is a question that has been the source of much debate for Christians. Although Peter gave an answer that seemed to be satisfactory for Jesus of Nazareth,[3] theologians have not been content with the answer. For many theologians, Peter's reply, "You are the Christ, the Son of the living God,"[4] begs for further explanation.

Theological disagreements regarding Jesus' identity reached a violent climax in the events leading up to the Council of Chalcedon. Nestorius and Cyril disagreed on the nature of Jesus Christ's incarnation and his relationship to his earthly mother Mary. Because of his belief in the distinctiveness of the two natures in the incarnate Word, Nestorius claimed that Mary could not be called the mother of God. Cyril of Alexandria, on the other hand, emphasized

---

[1] Professor Robert Benson of UCLA made helpful comments on this paper in 1992.
[2] Matthew 16:15b (NIV).
[3] Matthew 16:17 (NIV).
[4] Matthew 16:16 (NIV).

the union of two natures in the incarnation and, therefore, supported calling Mary the mother of God. These differences resulted in mutual accusation of heresy. Upon closer examination of Cyril's writings in light of the primitive Christian and earlier Patristic thinkers, one can see that Cyril's writings represent the orthodox position.

Nestorius had a serious problem with those who saw Mary as the mother of God. Nestorius comments:

> Does God have a mother? A Greek without reproach introducing mothers for the gods! Is Paul then a liar when he says of the deity of Christ, "without father, without mother, without genealogy"? Mary, my friend, did not give birth to the Godhead (for "what is born of flesh is flesh"). A creature did not produce him who is uncreatable. The Father has not just recently generated God the Logos from the Virgin (for "in the beginning was the Logos," as John says). A creature did not produce the Creator, rather she gave birth

to the human being, the instrument of the Godhead.[5]

Nestorius, therefore, believed that one could only refer to Mary as the mother of the humanity in Jesus Christ. This is further evident in Nestorius's second letter to Cyril, in which he writes:

> Everywhere in Holy Scripture, whenever mention is made of the saving dispensation of the Lord, what is conveyed to us is the birth and suffering not of the deity but of the humanity of Christ, so that by a more exact manner of speech the holy Virgin is called Mother of Christ, not Mother of God.[6]

For Nestorius, the distinction between the humanity and the divinity of Christ was important.

Nestorius perceived anyone who did not believe in the distinction of the two natures in Christ as falling into Arian and Apollinarian heresies. Nestorius writes in his first sermon against the *Theotokos*:

---

[5] Richard A. Norris (tr. and ed.), *The Christological Controversy* (Philadelphia: Fortress Press, 1980), 124-125.
[6] Norris, 137.

> Am I the only one who calls Christ "twofold"? Does he not call himself both a destroyable temple and God who raises it up? And if it was God who was destroyed--and let that blasphemy be shifted to the head of Arius!--the Lord would have said, "Destroy this God and in three days I will raise him up." If God died when consigned to the grave, the Gospel saying "Why do you seek to kill me, a man, who have spoken truth to you?" is meaningless. But Christ is not a mere man, O slanderer! No, he is at once God and man. If he were God alone, he would have needed, O Apollinaris, to say, "Why do you seek to destroy me, who am God, who have spoken the truth to you?" What, in fact, he says is, "Why do you seek to kill me, a man?"[7]

For Nestorius, there had to be two natures in the incarnate Christ because only the humanity in Christ could suffer death and not

---
[7] Norris, 129.

the divinity. The divinity was involved in resurrecting the dead humanity in Jesus. The two natures, therefore, functioned differently.

Cyril, however, did not approve of such separation of the two natures. In his second letter to Nestorius, Cyril emphasizes the importance of seeing the two natures as firmly united:

> We say that in an unspeakable and incomprehensible way, the Logos united to himself, in his hypostasis, flesh enlivened by a rational soul, and in this way became a human being and has been designated "Son of man." .... Furthermore, we say that while the natures which were brought together into a true unity were different, there is nevertheless, because of the unspeakable and unutterable convergence into unity, one Christ and one Son out of the two. This is the sense in which it is said that, although he existed and was born from the Father before the ages, he was born of a woman in his flesh.[8]

---

[8] Norris, 132-133.

Cyril felt that this hypostastic union of the Logos to the body is what prompted the church Fathers to refer to Mary as the mother of God. Cyril writes:

> Accordingly, they boldly called the holy Virgin "God's mother," not because the nature of the Logos or the deity took the start of its existence in the holy Virgin but because the holy body which was born of her, possessed as it was of a rational soul, and to which the Logos was hypostatistically united, is said to have had a fleshly birth.[9]

One can see that Cyril was concerned with the unity of the two natures.

These theological differences had a lasting impact on the history of the Christian church. Cyril tried to show Nestorius as a heretic by showing that Nestorius denied that Mary's child was God and that Christ was two persons--the son of God and the son of man.[10]

The accusation of heresy by Cyril against Nestorius is understandable in light

---

[9] Norris, 134-135.
[10] R. U. Sellers, *The Council of Chalcedon* (London: S.P.C.K., 1961), xi.

of the language Nestorius used to describe the incarnation. First of all, Nestorius preferred the word "conjunction" (συναφεια) rather than "union" (ενωσις) to describe the incarnation because he wanted to make lucid the distinction between the humanity and the divinity in Christ.[11] But "conjunction" implies that the incarnation was merely external and the union incomplete.

Furthermore, the language Nestorius utilized in order to describe the natures in Christ was nebulous. Nestorius used the word *prosopon* to describe the incarnate Christ and also the two natures of Christ which, he claimed, continued to exist individually even after the incarnation. Thus, the *prosopon* of the divinity, or the Word, and the *prosopon* of the humanity are not identical with the *prosopon* of the union. Rather, the *prosopon* of the union, as described above, is the result of the conjunction of the two natures.[12] Nestorius, therefore, pointed to an incomplete union with his emphasis on the distinctiveness of the two natures in Christ.

Cyril understood Nestorius' concept of the conjunction of the two natures as not being a union at all. Cyril felt that Nestorius was dividing Christ into the Word and an ordinary man and making incarnation a mere

---

[11] J. N. D. Kelly, *Early Christian Doctrines* (San Francisco: HarperSanFrancisco, 1978), 314.
[12] Kelly, 315.

illusion. Thus, the atoning death belonged merely to an ordinary human being, and not to the incarnate God. This, in effect, nullified the efficacious work of the Christ's propitiatory atonement. The Eucharist, therefore, ceased to be a sacrament, but rather a symbolic act of cannibalism. This was clearly a heresy in the eyes of Cyril.

J. N. D. Kelly offers an explanation for the difficulty that Nestorius faced. Nestorius' emphasis on the distinctiveness of the two natures did not allow him to clearly explain the nature of the incarnate Christ. Kelly comments:

> The real problem, however, especially for the one who set the independence and completeness of the natures so much in the foreground, was to explain what constituted His Person, the metaphysical subject of His being, and this Nestorius's theory hardly touched.[13]

Whatever his reasons might have been, Nestorius failed to clearly explain his position in a way acceptable to the Church. The end result was that he had a major heresy named after him.

---

[13] 317.

On the other hand, the Antiochene Christians and their bishop John felt that Cyril was the heretic. The Antiochene Christians were heirs of the Syrian school of thought which emphasized the difference between God the creator and man the creature and, also, the importance and reality of the humanity of the incarnate Logos for the purpose of human salvation.

Looking from this standpoint, John and the Antiochene Christians viewed Cyril's anathemas as heretical. They felt that Cyril was doing away with the Creator-creature distinction in making the divine Logos mutable and passable. Thus, they felt that Cyril was preaching one nature of Jesus Christ by identifying his human nature with his divine nature. For the Antiochene Christians, this idea proved dangerous in light of their belief that the humanity of the incarnate Son had to be real for human salvation.[14]

Cyril's fourth anathema did seem to confirm their fears. Cyril writes in his third letter to Nestorius:

> Car, même si le Verbe «*a habité parmi nous*» (Jo 1, 44) et s'il a été dit que «*toute la plénitude de la déité habite corporellement dans le Christ*» (Col 2, 9), nous

---

[14] Sellers, 8.

> concevons du moins que, une fois devenu chair, ce n'est pas en la façon dont il est dit habiter dans les saints, ce n'est pas de la même façon que nous définissons que l'habitation a eu lieu en lui, mais c'est unifié par nature et non changé dans la chair qu'il a rendu cette habitation de la même sorte que l'âme de l'homme serait dite avoir son habitation dans le corps qui lui est approprié.[15]

The analogy between the union of soul and body, and the union of the Word and man was inadequate in the eyes of the Antiochenes who believed that soul and body were incomplete and, therefore, united out of necessity. This is contrasted with Christ's union since it was a voluntary union of the perfect Word for the purpose of vicarious atonement for humans.[16] Therefore, Antiochenes presumed that Cyril was teaching the confusion of natures, which was a heresy.

Furthermore, the Antiochene Christians suspected Cyril of heresy since Cyril was loath to describe the incarnate Word as

---

[15] A. J. Festugière (tr.), *Éphèse et Chalcédoine: Actes des Conciles* (Paris: Beauchesne, 1982), 60. Italics Not Mine.
[16] Kelly, 313.

being in two natures. Paul Galtier describes the intensity of Cyril's reluctance: "...Cyrille s'etait toujours refusé à parler de deux natures distinctes après l'union...."[17] Cyril, therefore, did not like the phase, "in two natures" (εν δυο φυσεσι), because it pointed to the existence of two natures after incarnation. Cyril felt that this made the incarnation merely external, and, in turn, the incarnate Word would be no different from any of the saints or prophets.[18] Cyril's objection to talk about the two natures after the incarnation is consistent with his abhorrence of the Nestorian emphasis on the distinctiveness of the divine and human natures. Cyril was interested in describing only one nature of Jesus Christ; that is, the nature of the incarnation.[19] But the Antiochenes misunderstood Cyril as doing away with the human nature and making the divine nature mutable and passable, so they accused Cyril of being a heretic.

The case of Eutyches seemed to confirm their apprehension regarding Cyril's emphasis on one nature of the incarnate

---

[17] "Saint Cyrille d'Alexandrie et Saint Léon le Grand à Chalcédoine," Aloys Grillmeier and Heinrich Bacht (ed.), *Das Konzil von Chalkedon: Geschichte und Gegenwart* (Würzburg: Echter-Verlag Würzburg, 1951, 345-387), 355.
[18] V. C. Samuel, *The Council of Chalcedon Reexamined: A Historical and Theological Survey* (Madras: The Christian Literature Society, 1977), 11.
[19] Galtier, 371.

Word. The radical emphasis on the one nature of the incarnate Word brought troubles for Eutyches. On September 8, 448, Eusebius of Dorylaeum in Phrygia declared before the Home Synod in Constantinople that he was prepared to show Eutyches as a heretic.[20] Against his own wishes, Eutyches appeared before the synod to defend his faith, when Flavian, at the fifth session, demanded his physical presence.[21] Eutyches avowed belief in the two natures before the incarnation. But when Eutyches could not answer in the affirmation to the question of belief in the two natures after the incarnation, he met his condemnation. Galtier records the account:

> «Oui», venait de répondre l'archimandrite, «j'admets l'union εκ δυο φυσεων». -- «Mais», avait repris Eusèbe, «confess-tu, oui ou non, deux natures, après l'incarnation?» Et c'est pour s'être obstinément refusé à cette confession qu'Eutychès avait été condamné.[22]

Eutyches represented an example of extreme adherence to Cyril's doctrine of one nature.

---

[20] Sellers, 57.
[21] Sellers, 63-64.
[22] 363.

One might assume from the case of Eutyches that Cyril's views might have bordered on heresy, too, since Eutyches was claiming to be defending the Alexandrian position. But this would not be accurate. Upon closer examination, one will notice that Cyril would not have agreed with Eutyches' stance. Although Cyril emphasized the union of the two natures into one nature of the incarnate Word, the incarnate nature, in Cyril's mind, existed in two parts -- divine and human, in a distinct way. This can be seen in Cyril's letters to the monks:

> Ainsi donc, de l'aveu de tous, l'Emmanuel est composé de deux éléments, la déité et l'humanité. Cependant l'unique Seigneur Jésus-Christ, qui est véritablement Fils unique, est tout ensemble Dieu et homme, et il n'est pas un homme déifié comme le sont les hommes déifiés par grâce, mais il est plutôt Dieu vrai qui est apparu parmi nous sous forme humaine.[23]

This passage shows that Cyril was concerned with the two natures--divine and human--within the one incarnate Jesus Christ. Thus, despite Cyril's emphasis on

---

[23] Festugière, 38.

the one nature of Jesus after incarnation and his preference for the use of the term "from two natures" over the one accepted at Chalcedon, "in two natures," it is safe to presume that Cyril was in agreement with the orthodox faith that stressed two natures within the one incarnate Christ.

Furthermore, Galtier shows that the Chalcedon language describing the distinctiveness of Christ's two natures belonged to Cyril:

> À tout propos et de toutes les manières il le repète: dans l'union, la nature divine reste immutable et la nature humaine y est ce qu'elle est en chacun de nous. Pas de mélange ni de confusion: les adverbes de Chalcédoine ασυγχυτως, ατρεπτως sont de lui.[24]

One can see that despite his emphasis on the language of the one nature of the incarnate Logos to avoid the Nestorian heresy, Cyril was further interested in keeping the divine and human natures apart within the one incarnate Christ--without mixture nor confusion.

The orthodoxy in Cyril's thoughts can be found further in his ideas concerning

---

[24] 366.

the relationship of the incarnate Word to the human salvation. Cyril used the phrase, "from two natures" (εκ δυο φυσεων), to describe the incarnation of the Word because he believed that the incarnate Christ was the result of the coming together of the two natures--human and divine--in a hypostastic way. The Word remained the same before and after the incarnation. But what happened in the incarnation is that the Word, who existed outside of the human body (ασαρκος), became embodied (ενσωματος).[25] And the embodied Word is one in nature; that is, the incarnate nature.

The oneness of the incarnate Word was of chief importance to Cyril because of its soteriological implications. God himself became incarnated and took the form of humans in Jesus Christ so that when Jesus died, God in his incarnate form participated in the death and resurrection.[26] Such participation of the divine made the atoning sacrifice of Jesus Christ effective and gave legitimacy to the Eucharist. This is why Cyril was careful to emphasize the one incarnate nature of Jesus Christ and the phrase, "from two natures." Cyril felt that Nestorius' emphasis on the distinctiveness of two natures and his description of the incarnation as mere conjunction, rather than a union, denigrated the salvific work of the

---

[25] Kelly, 319.
[26] Kelly, 321.

incarnate Word and stripped him of his glory. For Cyril, it was important that God was involved personally in the atoning death.

Great Christian thinkers before Cyril confirmed Cyril's orthodoxy by attesting the importance of the involvement of the divine in the atoning death. One example from the primitive church was Paul of Tarsus. After all, Paul proclaimed the glory of Jesus Christ in his humility: although he possessed divine nature, he humbled himself by taking on the human nature and further humbled himself by participating in a death by a cross. It is found in Philippians 2:5-11:

> Your attitude should be the same as that of Christ Jesus: Who being in very nature God, did not consider equality with God something to be grasped, but made himself nothing, taking the very nature of a servant, being made in human likeness. And being found in appearance as a man, he humbled himself and became obedient to death--even death on a cross! Therefore God exalted him to the highest place and gave him the name that is above every name, that at the

name of Jesus every knee should bow, in heaven and on earth and under the earth, and every tongue confess that Jesus Christ is Lord, to the glory of God the Father.[27]

One can see that the beauty of Christ's humiliation consisted in the ultimate humility of a divine being taking a human nature and participating in the most shameful death possible in the Roman empire. And most scholars of the early Christian history believe that Philippians 2:6-11 was a psalm that was commonly sung or read in the primitive church to teach its members basic theology and provide an apologetic tool for them.[28] This shows that it was important for the primitive church that Jesus Christ, who is God, took a human form and participated in the atoning death on a cross. It was their central belief. And in a tradition that emphasizes apostolic succession, one should not be surprised that such emphasis on Christology passed down.

And one can find in the writings of the church fathers the emphasis that God had to participate in death through the human nature he has taken in Christ.

---

[27] (NIV).
[28] Wayne A. Meeks, *The First Urban Christians: The Social World of the Apostle Paul* (New Haven: Yale University Press, 1983), 144.

Tertullian, a Latin-speaking North African, writes against Marcion in "On the Flesh of Christ":

> But answer me this, you murderer of truth: Was not God truly crucified? And being truly crucified, did he not truly die? And having truly died, was he not truly raised? .... In what way will these things hold true of [Christ] if he himself was not true, if he did not truly have what it takes to be crucified, to die, to be buried, and to be raised--that is , this flesh of ours, suffused with blood, built up on bones, woven through with sinews, intertwined with veins?[29]

This passage shows that Tertullian, like the primitive Christians, was concerned with the incarnate God actually dying on a cross. Tertullian, therefore, stressed that God had to have flesh to die.

Origen, who belonged to the Greek Christian tradition and was the successor of Clement of Alexandria as the head of the catechetical school at Alexandria in Egypt, agreed with Tertullian in that the Son of God

---

[29] Norris, 69-70.

suffered death since he was united with his human flesh capable of death. Origen writes:

> Conversely, the Son of God, through whom all things were created, is named Jesus Christ and Son of Man. For the Son of God is said to have died, by virtue, to be sure, of the nature which is truly capable of sustaining death.[30]

This is in agreement also with Cyril's emphasis that the God in the incarnate Word participated in death.

In the fourth century, Athanasius wrote an apologetic treaties on Christology. His ideas resembled closely with Cyril's beliefs. Like Cyril, Athanasius refered to Mary as the God-bearer. Athanasius writes in his "Orations against the Arians": "Furthermore, it [Scriptures] says that in the end he [the Logos] became a human being, he took flesh for our sakes from the Virgin Mary, the God-bearer."[31]

Furthermore, Cyril's belief in the hypostastic union of the Word closely resembled Athanasius' view on the union of the two natures. The union was not mere

---

[30] Norris, 76.
[31] Norris, 87.

external conjunction, but rather an intricate and perfect union. Athanasius writes in the same treatise:

> He became human. He did not enter into a human being. It is, moreover, crucial to recognize this. Otherwise, these impious people might fall into this error too and deceive some others, and these in their turn might suppose that just as in earlier times the Logos "came to be" in each of the saints, so even now he came into residence in a human being, sanctifying this one also and being revealed just as he was in others.[32]

Even the Athanasian criticism of the view that the incarnation is like the Word descending on the saints resounds in Cyril's fourth anathema.

Athanasius, as with the rest of the orthodox fathers and Cyril, believed that the divine in the incarnated Christ took part in the redeeming death on the cross. Athanasius wrote in his "Orations against the Arians":

---

[32] Norris, 88.

Consequently, when the flesh was suffering, the Logos was not apart from it. That is why the suffering also is said to belong to him. .... If...the flesh belongs to the Logos (for "the Logos became flesh"), it is necessary to predicate the fleshly passions of him whose flesh it is. And the one of whom the passions are predicated -- condemnation, for example, scourging and crucifixion and death and the other weaknesses of the body -- is also the one to whom the triumph and the grace are attributed. So it is logical and fitting that passions of this sort be predicated not of another but of the Lord, in order that grace also may derive from him and we may become not worshipers of someone else but truly servants of God.[33]

One can see the importance Athanasius placed on the involvement of the divine in the salvific work of Jesus Christ. This survey of Christian thinkers clearly show Cyril to be the orthodox thinker.

---

[33] Norris, 90-91.

Historical Implications of Nestorius

The fifth century saw the clash of two main Christologies. Nestorius emphasized the existence of the two natures after the incarnation. For him, the Creator-creature distinction had to be intact. Therefore, Mary could not be called the mother of God; rather, merely, the mother of the humanity within the incarnate Word. He was dogmatic in his beliefs to the extent that he emphasized that the divine in Jesus Christ did not participate in the atoning death on a cross. He claimed that God could not die and accused Cyril of mixing and confusing the two natures in the incarnate Word. Yet, Nestorius and his followers, like the Antiochenes and John, misunderstood Cyril. Cyril, in fact, did believe in the distinctiveness of the divinity and humanity in the incarnate Word. This is attested in his writings as well as in the fact that key words, such as "without mixture or confusion," belong to Cyril. Yet, to stress the importance of understanding the incarnate Word as one and not composed of two different beings, like the son of God and the son of man, Cyril of Alexandria emphasized oneness of the incarnate Logos. But Cyril's orthodoxy is uncontested in light of writers from the primitive and earlier patristic church.

Bibliography

Festugière, A. J. (tr.). *Éphèse et Chalcédoine: Actes des Conciles.* Paris: Beauchesne, 1982.

Grillmeier, Aloys, and Heinrich Bacht (ed.). *Das Konzil von Chalkedon: Geschichte und Gegenwart.* Würzburg: Echter-Verlag Würzburg, 1951.

Kelly, J. N. D. *Early Christian Doctrines.* San Francisco: HarperSanFrancisco, 1978.

Meeks, Wayne A. *The First Urban Christians: The Social World of the Apostle Paul.* New Haven: Yale University Press, 1983.

Norris, Richard A. (tr. and ed.). *The Christological Controversy.* Philadelphia: Fortress Press, 1980.

Samuel, V. C. *The Council of Chalcedon Re-examined: A Historical and Theological Survey.* Madras: The Christian Literature Society, 1977.

Sellers, R. U. *The Council of Chalcedon.* London: S. P. C. K., 1961.

The Holy Bible: New International Version. Colorado Springs: International Bible Society, 1984.

Gospel of John's Son of Man: Communal Self-Definition in Motion[1]

In the context of the growing rift with an actively self-defining Judaism, the Gospel of John acts as a document describing a community's effort to exist and define itself with the cultic figure, Jesus of Nazareth, at the center. Central to the question of the legitimacy of the community is the claim that Jesus of Nazareth was the legitimate envoy of God. Such apologetic tendency is nowhere more poignant in the gospel than in the "son of man" sayings attributed to the lips of Jesus himself. The son of man language is wrapped in the powerful imagery of heavenly origin and return, of being "lifted up" and of being glorified. A careful examination of four texts, 3.13, 6.62, 8.28, and 20.17, in the backdrop of other son of man references and passages that contain the poignant imageries already mentioned above will serve to enlighten

---

[1] This paper was written at the Hebrew University of Jerusalem in Israel. I would like to thank Professor Marinus de Jonge of Holland's Leiden University, who was a visiting professor at the Hebrew University of Jerusalem. Professor de Jonge kindly read the complete draft of the paper and offered many helpful comments and gave kind encouragements.

Johannine Christology in its socio-historical context.

The Gospel of John depicts a situation in which the claims of a community which claimed Jesus of Nazareth as the legitimate envoy of God[2] has caused a rift with the dominant Judaism which sought to define what it meant to be a Jew.[3] This is nowhere more clear than in chapter 9. In verse 22, it is stated: "His parents said this because they were afraid of the Jews, for already the Jews had decided that anyone who acknowledged that Jesus was the Christ would be put out of the synagogue" (NIV). The parents of the man born blind avoided

---

[2] Painter argues that the Gospel of John is a self-conscious reinterpretation of messiahship in light of the evangelist's understanding of Jesus. Furthermore, the quest for the Messiah is reinterpreted as the quest for life -- eternal life (*The Quest for the Messiah: The History, Literature and Theology of the Johannine Community* (Nashville: Abingdon Press, 1993) 9).

[3] In 70 AD., the Romans destroyed the Jerusalem Temple and passed on the leadership of Judaism to the Pharisees. Although the Pharisees had been influential in the Diaspora, the existence of the Temple and the cultus within had provided the Sadducees with the leadership. But with the Temple cultus gone, the Pharisees, who placed greater emphasis on the Law than on the no-longer available redemptive media of the Temple and the Land as the Sadducees did, were able to seize the leadership in Jamnia and began to define Judaism. At the center of this definition was the Eighteen Benedictions, a central prayer that was to become fixed and standard.

identifying Jesus as the healer of their son and told "the Jews" to ask their son to identify the healer (vv. 21, 23) because they feared expulsion from the synagogue, as is stipulated in the twelfth[4] of the Eighteen Benedictions for the *minim*, or heretics, and the *Nazarim*, seen as Christians. John 9:22 is significant in that it shows that not only was there a knowledge of this decision in the *Sitz im Leben* of the Johannine community, but also a real reason for fear; the policy of exclusion must have been practiced. In this context, the purpose of the Gospel of John can be easily understood as an effort to encourage the Christian believers to have courage for faith in Jesus Christ in the midst of a real fear and for those who have left or were forced out of the synagogues to hold securely to their decision to profess Jesus as the messiah.

This encouragement is found even in chapter 9 in the witness of the healed man. In John 9:35b, Jesus of Nazareth asks the healed man: "Do you believe in the Son of Man?" (NIV). The once-blind man's response to this question is significant; he replied by asking: "Who is he, sir? .... Tell me so that I may believe in him" (v. 36 NIV). One quickly notices that the man did not ask: "What is the son of man?" One, therefore, understands from this that the

---

[4]Painter dates the publication of *birkat hamminim* at around 85 AD. (76).

term "son of man" was quite widely known and understood as a messianic term.[5] Jesus identifies himself as the son of man (v. 37), and the healed man responds in profession of belief and worships him (v. 38). This expression of faith is significant especially in the context of the chapter. Previously stated was the passage showing that the confession of Jesus as the Christ was the reason for expulsion from the synagogue. Nonetheless, the man born blind believes in Jesus. Surely, this was to show those believers wavering in the synagogues to stand firm in their faith. There are others who also knew the consequences of standing firm in their faith in Jesus as the messiah but, nevertheless, professed their faith and faced expulsion. But this was presumably more

---

[5]Identification of Jesus of Nazareth as the Danielic son of man is clearly evident in John 5:27, which J. Louis Martyn believes to be the most "traditional" son of man saying in the whole of the New Testament (*History and Theology in the Fourth Gospel* (Nashville: Abingdon, 1979) 139). John 5:27 states that the Father, namely God the Father, has given to the Son, namely Jesus Christ, the authority to judge because the Son is the son of man. The Danielic son of man is an apocalyptic judge, and Jesus receives this right to judge as the prophetic fulfillment of the Danielic son of man. This passage points to the understanding of the term, "son of man," as messianic in the *Sitz im Leben* of the Johannine community. Painter states that the understanding of son of man as a figure to be worshipped is distinctively Johannine (305).

than worthwhile because of Jesus' special identity as the true envoy of God.

In the Gospel of John, heavenly origin and return constitute integral components of his identity. Jesus of Nazareth, as the son of man, was sent[6] by God for a specific purpose; therefore, he does nothing except the will of God. Jesus is able to do what God the Father[7] wants because he has a "direct-line" with God as the Son of God.[8] And Jesus glorifies the Father by what he

---

[6] John Ashton argues that the son of man in the Gospel of John was not sent from heaven: "If the Son of Man were indeed *sent* then he would have to be thought of as sent from heaven. But this point is not made. The Son of Man is first of all not an emissary but an intermediary" (*Understanding of the Fourth Gospel* (Oxford: Clarendon Press, 1991) 348. Italics Not Mine). Ashton's statement contradicts the Johannine motif of the heavenly origin and return of the son of man, which will be discussed throughout the paper.

[7] Painter warns against anachronistically reading fullblown Trinitarian debates back into the gospel because the Johannine Christological development has as its source Jewish messianic expectations and wisdom speculation and lacks the precision of later definitions (31).

[8] Marinus de Jonge believes that the central titles in John are "son of man" and "Son of God." Son of God is particularly an offensive title for the Jews of the gospel, as evidenced by John 19:7, in which the Jews are described as insisting: "We have a law, and according to that law he must die, because he claimed to be the Son of God" (NIV) (*Christology in Context: The Earliest Christian Response to Jesus* (Philadelphia: The Westminster Press, 1988) 145).

does and is in turn glorified by the Father for such obedient behavior. Jesus' return to his place of origin finds consummation in his death on the cross. Jesus is "lifted up" on the cross physically but this finds parallel in his existential exaltation, or glorification.[9] Jesus of Nazareth's authority, therefore, supersedes that of any previous great figures in Judaism, even Moses.[10] Thus, one can see that the Gospel of John functioned as an apologia against those who were persecuting them, but also as a reassurance for its members who had been separated, sometimes forcibly, from the synagogues and mainstream Judaism and as encouragement for those who hesitated avowing their beliefs by staying in the synagogues to profess their faith.

Such a tenet of the Johannine community could not but find problems within the socio-historical context of an actively self-defining Judaism. Any kind of strong sectarian cultic figure poses problems for a mainstream movement. The Qumran com-

---

[9] Such qualities attributed to Jesus of Nazareth provided a point of departure from other contemporaneous miracle workers who had a following, such as Hanina ben Doza and Honi the Circle Drawer.

[10] Martyn believes that the Gospel of John has a two tier typological identification of Jesus -- first as the Mosaic Prophet-Messiah and then shortly after as the son of man. The identity of Jesus as the son of man, however, occupies the central stage in the gospel (134-135).

munity[11] provides an example. The Teacher of Righteousness followed a strict interpretation of the Torah, but such interpretation differed from that of the leadership in Jerusalem; thus, he was forced into the desert with a small following. The expulsion of Johannine Christians can be seen in a similar light. Jews who brazenly followed the cultic figure, Jesus of Nazareth, were forced out of the synagogues, because their claims posed a disturbance to the Pharisaic leadership which had as its task definition of post-Temple Destruction Jewish identity. It was a conservative leadership, which saw, at the single stroke of the Romans, the disappearance of their major competition. It now looked for stability and conservative construction and development. Thus, the Johannine Christians needed strong arguments for the legitimacy of Jesus of Nazareth.

Indeed, four passages to be examined in this paper (John 3:13; 6:62; 8:28; 20:17), provide evidence of the Johannine argument for the legitimacy of Jesus of Nazareth as the true envoy of God and involve powerful

---

[11] The Qumran community and its texts provide evidence of syncretistic and "sectarian" nature of first century Palestinian Judaism. The fact that the Qumran community developed themes and ideas based on the Old Testament different from those of the "mainstream" Judaism supports the argument that the Johannine community possibly believed that their faith in Jesus Christ arose from legitimate Jewish messianic expectations (Painter 50-51).

imagery of heavenly origin and return, of being "lifted up," and of being glorified.

The first passage, John 3:13, attributes legitimacy of Jesus of Nazareth by pointing to his heavenly origin. The passage reads: "No one has ever gone into heaven except the one who came from heaven -- the Son of Man" (NIV). In the context of John the Baptist's testimony about Jesus (John 3:27ff.), this verse clearly stands out as a confirmation of Jesus' authority.[12] Particularly in verse 31, John the Baptist is described as saying: "The one who comes from above is above all; the one who is from the earth belongs to the earth, and speaks as one from earth. The one who comes from heaven is above all" (NIV). This is a part of the response that John the Baptist gave to his disgruntled disciples, who were jealous of Jesus' baptizing ministry which was attractting "everyone" (v. 26). Not only did John the Baptist support Jesus' ministry, but he also believed it to be the norm that Jesus became greater and that he became lesser in ministry (v. 30). For Jesus, sent by God, speaks the word of God (v. 34), and those who believe in the Son have eternal life (v.

---

[12]Painter believes that John 3:13 may be understood as a polemic against the claim that Moses ascended to heaven and came back with heavenly knowledge. The evangelist, wanting to elevate Jesus' authority above all, including Moses, asserts that the son of man first descended and reascended because he is a heavenly figure (330).

36). This statement regarding the receiving of eternal life based on belief in the Son, as placed on the lips of John the Baptist, supports the concept of receiving eternal life for belief in the son of man found in verses 14-15: "Just as Moses lifted up the snake in the desert, so the Son of Man must be lifted up, that everyone who believes in him may have eternal life" (NIV). Thus, the heavenly origin of the son of man functions as legitimization of Jesus' ministry and authority; therefore, it is not surprising that the Gospel of John describes the salvation of the faithful as the purpose for which God sent his Son (John 3:16-17), identified in the Gospel of John as Jesus of Nazareth.

The concept of descent-ascent of Jesus finds multiple attestation in Ephesians 4:8-10. In verse 8, the author of Ephesians quotes Psalm 68:18 as a verse that prophetically describes Jesus Christ. In explanatory statements in the following two verses, the writer takes it as a truism that the phrase "he ascended" quoted from Psalm 68:18 also points to the descent of Christ: "What does 'he ascended' mean except that he also descended to the lower, earthly regions? He who descended is the very one who ascended higher than all the heavens, in order to fill the whole universe" (vv. 9-10 NIV). One notices that this concept is directly parallel to the idea found in John 3:13 -- one who ascended to heaven is the one who already descended to earth. Both John 3:13 and Ephesians 4:8-10 support the concept of heavenly origin and return of Jesus.

The second passage, John 6:62, is also a descent-ascent son of man passage; Jesus is quoted as saying: "What if you see the Son of Man ascend to where he was before?" (NIV). This is the third and last son of man passage in the series of son of man passages that form a logical whole in chapter 6. To better understand the import of the descent-ascent son of man passage in verse 62 as legitimization of the ministry and authority of the son of man, or Jesus of Nazareth, one needs to examine the first two son of man passages in their context.

The first passage, John 6:27, is found in the context of Jesus of Nazareth rebuking the crowd for seeking him as the result of the miraculous feeding work that he performed. Jesus encourages them to seek food that does not spoil, namely that which the son of man will give them. The eternal quality of this food is dependent on the legitimacy of the son of man, on whom God the Father, according to the second half of John 6:27, has placed his seal of approval.

In response to Jesus' statement not to work for food that spoils, but rather for food that endures eternally, the crowd asks Jesus in verse 28 how they may arrive at doing the works that God requires. In verse 29, Jesus responds by saying that the will of God is for them to believe in the one whom he has sent, referring to himself. Then, the crowd demands another miraculous sign, so that they may believe (v. 30). They give as an example of a miraculous sign the manna that their forefathers ate (v. 31). They called the manna, "bread from heaven." This demand for another miraculous sign is strange in light of the previous feeding miracle. The feeding of the five thousand, accounted in John 6:1ff., surely parallels the manna feeding in the desert by which masses of Israelites were fed.

    Jesus of Nazareth responds to such a demand by stating that it was not Moses who gave bread from heaven, but rather God the Father, called "my Father" in verse 32, who gives true bread from heaven. And this "true bread from heaven" takes on a metaphorical meaning; for, the bread is the individual who comes down from heaven and gives life to the world. Jesus then claims in verse 35 that he is the bread of life and the source of eternal satisfaction of hunger and thirst.

    Jesus says that he came down from heaven to do the will of "him who sent me" rather than his own will (v. 38). And this will is that Jesus will not lose any that were sent by the Father, but rather to raise them up at the last day (v. 39). For the Father wills that all who look to the Son and believe in him will have eternal life (v. 40).

Here, one is reminded of the typology in John 3:14 in which the son of man acts as the anti-type of the snake of salvation which Moses lifted up in the desert, with the result that all the Israelites who looked at it were delivered from their capital punishment.

Jesus' revelation of himself as the bread from heaven met with a negative reaction from the Jews; they point to Jesus' parents, whom they knew, and question how Jesus could make such an outrageous statement (vv. 41-2). One notices that the audience has narrowed to "the Jews" from "the crowd." To such negative response of the Jews, Jesus responded with a repetitive explication of his metaphoric identity as the bread from heaven and of his mission (vv. 43-51). But one factor stands out as a great, new revelation; this bread from heaven which grants eternal life is his own flesh. The response of the Jews is perhaps a natural one; they ask how Jesus may give his flesh for them to eat (v. 52).

Then comes the second son of man saying in chapter 6. In verse 53, Jesus of Nazareth states: "I tell you the truth, unless you eat the flesh of the Son of Man and drink his blood, you have no life in you" (NIV). Here, one notices the change in tone. Previously, Jesus of Nazareth stated his identity and mission and sought to explain it -- perhaps with the purpose of convincing his audience. The basic proposition, therefore, was: if you do, you will receive; namely, I am the bread of life and those who believe in me will have eternal life. But now, the basic proposition is: if you do not do, you do/will not have; namely, if you do not eat the flesh and drink the blood of the son of man, you have no life in you. This negative proposition, however, follows a positive explicative, parallel statement: whoever eats Jesus' flesh and drinks his blood has eternal life (v. 54). One quickly notices that the personal, first person, singular pronoun, "I," of Jesus in verse 54 parallels the son of man of verse 53. Thus, verses 53 to 58 function as a speech restating Jesus of Nazareth's identity and mission.

Jesus stresses feeding on him as a means to eternal life because he is the bread from heaven. Thus, one understands that the bread which the son of man would give "that endures to eternal life" (v. 27) is in fact Jesus the son of man himself. He would give himself. Jesus' argument is capsulated in verses 57-58: "Just as the living Father sent me and I live because of the Father, so the one who feeds on me will live because of me. This is the bread that came down from heaven. Your forefathers ate manna and died, but he who feeds on this bread will live forever" (NIV). This mystical language, taken on face value, seems more than outrageous; it sounds like cannibalism. Thus, the negative response of "the Jews" is followed by that of Jesus' own disciples.

According to verse 60, "many" of Jesus' disciples responds to Jesus' claim to legitimacy and explication of his mission in unbelief: "This is a hard teaching. Who can accept it?" (NIV). This becomes the prelude to the last son of man message in chapter 6. Jesus asks them first if this teaching of his offends them (v. 61). Then, Jesus says: "What if you see the Son of Man ascend to where he was before?" (v. 62 NIV). Underlying this statement is the presumption that his disciples would believe should they see him ascend to where he was before. Further implicit in this statement is the concept of the descent and ascent of the son of man. Jesus is here taking for granted the descent of the son of man and rhetorically asks them if they would believe if he ascends back to the place of his origin, namely heaven.

Then, Jesus of Nazareth interjects a Gnostic-sounding[13] statement: "The Spirit gives life, the flesh counts for nothing. The

---

[13]The letters of John shows the Sitz im Leben of the Johannine community at a later time. A group of Johannine Christians, who argued that the Son of God did not have a real body of flesh and blood, separated from the group which writes 1 John and from the elder who writes 2 and 3 John (I John 2:19; 2 John 7-11). Implicit in I John 2:20-27 is the claim by both sides of the conflict that they were led by the spirit and possess true knowledge (de Jonge 143-144).

words I have spoken to you are spirit and they are life" (v. 63 NIV). Here, one sees that the spirit is contrasted dualistically with the flesh and is superimposed over it; spirit is good, flesh is bad. Then, Jesus equates his words as spirit and life. It is a gnosis -- a special knowledge that grants one entrance to eternal life. This seen in light of his reference to himself as the bread of heaven surely points one to interpret the feeding of his flesh in a mystical light. And surely the Last Supper references in the Gospel and the Eucharistic account of Paul clarifies this as a Eucharistic reference, pointing to the mission of Jesus.

According to the text, Jesus of Nazareth recognizes that some of his disciples did not believe (v. 64a), and according to the narrative, Jesus knew from "the beginning" who did not believe and who would betray him (v. 64b). Then, Jesus comments that no one could "come" to him unless the Father allows the person (v. 65). Here, one sees predestinarian thinking. Some of you do not believe because you were not chosen by God to believe. The gnosis is, therefore, closed to you.

According to John 6:66, many disciples ceased to follow Jesus of Nazareth. The question remains whether it was the specific teaching of the feeding that compelled them to leave or whether it was Jesus' claim that only those whom the Father allows to understand will understand -- thus, those who did not understand took offense and left. But the end result of their desertion of Jesus is the important point of the account. For Jesus says to his twelve disciples in verse 67: "You do not want to leave too, do you?" (NIV).

At this point it is important to note that the account in chapter 6 does not merely point to a reality in Jesus' ministry but also describes the *Sitz im Leben* of the Johannine community. The teaching that Jesus of Nazareth was the one sent by God and that he descended from and then ascended to heaven, to the presence of God, was offensive and even dangerous to the Jewish leadership that tried to define the identity of Judaism. A cultic leader, a dead one, who roused dissension in the synagogues was not what they needed. Thus, harsh sentence, namely expulsion from the synagogues for the followers of Jesus, prompted some of the believers to renounce their faith. There is a two tier denial: first, "the Jews" embodied in the leadership opposes Jesus and following him, then some of "the believers" denounce their faith in Jesus.

Thus, for those who remain in the Johannine community or, rather, actively join the Johannine community receive courage from such predestinarian thinking: they are the chosen ones. They have the gnosis. Others fell away because they were not chosen by God to enter into knowledge. Jesus of Nazareth is indeed the one sent by God, having come from heaven and having returned back there. We feed on him through the Eucharist and thus will endure to eternal life. These ideas granted the member of the Johannine community the courage to stay within the community. Furthermore, such ideas functioned as encouragement to the wavering believers of Jesus within the synagogues to proclaim their faith and bravely face expulsion.

      The third passage presents itself in John 8:28, in the background context of Jesus' self-proclamation as the "light of the world" (v. 12). Immediately, the Pharisees challenge Jesus' claim by stating that Jesus' claim is not valid by virtue of the fact that he testified about himself (v. 13). Jesus does not deny that he testified about himself, but he does affirm the validity of his claim. Jesus argues that the legitimacy of his claim hinges on the nature of his identity. Jesus claims that his testimony is valid even if he testifies about himself because he knows from where he came and to where he will return. Furthermore, Jesus states that his avowal is legitimate because his testimony has another witness besides himself; that is, the Father. Thus, the existence of two witnesses -- namely, Jesus and the Father -- allows the claim to be valid (vv. 14-18).

Then, Jesus tells the Pharisees that they will die in their sin and not go to where he will be going, heaven (v. 21), because they do not know him or the Father, especially since if they knew him they would know the Father through him (v. 19). Jesus claims that he is from above and the audience, the Jews, are from below (v. 23). And he reminds the Jews again that if they do not believe that Jesus is the one he claims to be, then they would die in their sins (v. 24). In response to this, the Jews ask Jesus who he is (v. 25a). At this question, Jesus responds as if the answer is obvious: "Just what I have been claiming all along" (v. 25b. NIV). Then, Jesus refers to the "reliable one" who sent him and tells the Jews that he tells "the world" what he has heard from him (v. 26). Here, his claim to legitimacy is surely based on his origin and the resultant communication with the Father.

But the Jews of the passage are portrayed as having missed the point. They did not know that Jesus was telling them about the Father (v. 27). Thus, Jesus responds: "When you have lifted up the Son of Man, then you will know that I am the one I claim to be and that I do nothing on my own but speak just what the Father has taught me" (v. 28. NIV). Thus, one sees the next son of man passage. In this passage, one sees the lifting up of the son of man as a source of legitimization. This passage, in an extended interpretation, can be seen as referring to the exaltation, or the glorification, of Jesus of Nazareth. But, most likely, it referred to the physical lifting up -- onto the cross. One must, however, notice that this physical lifting up of Jesus onto the cross parallels God's lifting him up in an existential glorification. De Jonge believes that the cross, in fact, is essential for Jesus' glorification: "As in the Synoptic Gospels, the Son of man has to die; the cross is, however, for John an essential element in the process of Jesus' being 'lifted up' (his 'glorification')."[14] This is evident in several Johannine son of man passages related with Jesus' death on the cross.

One such passage, which uses the language of "lifting up," is John 3:14, which states: "Just as Moses lifted up the snake in the desert, so the Son of Man must be lifted up"[15] (NIV). Thus, the son of man is the anti-type of the bronze snake (Numbers 21:8-9), which brought salvation for Israelites who were under capital punishment of God. In a similar way, Jesus functions as the source of salvation. Here, one sees the image of Jesus lifted up on the cross and dying; his death is the source of salvation. All who put their trust in him will see redemption, just as all those Israelites who

---

[14] 145.
[15] The necessity (δει) of the son of man's death is found in previous old Christian traditions, such as Mark 8:31 (Martyn 135).

looked up toward the snake in faith received deliverance from death. Thus, the cross is seen as a positive symbol[16] -- that of salvation.

Not only does Jesus' being lifted up onto the cross symbolize a source of salvation for believers, it further marks the process of Jesus' glorification. John 12:23 reads: "The hour has come for the Son of Man to be glorified" (NIV). Which hour was Jesus referring to? In the following verses, one sees that Jesus was pointing to his coming death on the cross. Jesus says: "I tell you the truth, unless a kernel of wheat falls to the ground and dies, it remains only a single seed. But if it dies, it produces many seeds" (v. 24 NIV). The single kernel points to Jesus, so that his death is shown to bring life to those who put their trust in him.

The fact that the son of man's glorification parallels his death is further affirmed in verse 27, in which Jesus is recorded as saying: "Now my heart is troubled, and what shall I say? 'Father, save me from this hour?' No, it was for this very reason I came to this hour" (NIV). Here, Jesus shows that

---

[16]Ashton notes that it is precisely the Johannine reluctance to see the crucifixion as demeaning or degrading that provides a contrast with the synoptists. The Greek word used, υψουν ("to raise" or "to elevate"), suggests a positive perception. In the Septuagint version of the story of Moses and the Bronze snake, the word used is ισταναι and not υψουν (364-365).

he is willing to face death and, in fact, it was for this that he came. For Jesus' death will bring glory to the Father's name (v. 28a). After Jesus requests the glorification of the name of the Father, one witnesses the following response. A voice responds: "I have glorified it, and will glorify it again" (v. 28b NIV). Jesus points out that the voice was for the benefit of the crowd (v. 30). Then, Jesus explains that he will be lifted up from the earth, thereby returning to his place of origin, with the result that he will draw "all men" to himself (v. 32). Thus, one sees that Jesus' death is the beginning of the process by which he will return to the place of his origin, namely heaven.

Another son of man passage which portrays the crucifixion as Jesus' glorifycation is John 13:31, in which Jesus is recorded as saying: "Now is the Son of Man glorified and God is glorified in him" (NIV). This verse must be seen in the context of the paragraph, the nature of which is the prediction of his death. Thus, Jesus says in verse 33: "My children, I will be with you only a little longer. You will look for me, and just as I told the Jews, so I tell you now: Where I am going, you cannot come" (NIV). As previously stated, Jesus will return to the place from which he came, namely heaven. He is from above. Thus, his disciples cannot come. But, unlike the crowd that did not believe, his true disciples will follow after

Jesus at a later time, even though not now (v. 36).

God is glorified in the son of man because the son carries out the mission for which he was sent by him, and in turn he glorifies the Son. Jesus states: "If God is glorified in him, God will glorify the Son in himself, and will glorify him at once" (v. 32 NIV). When one combines this verse with verse 31, one notices that the "son of man" of verse 31 parallels the "Son" of verse 32. Thus, in verse 32, the missing agent of the son of man's glorification in verse 31 is known; that is, God.

The fourth passage for examination and of great importance is John 20:17, in which Jesus is recorded as having said: "Do not hold on to me, for I have not yet returned to the Father. Go instead to my brothers and tell them, 'I am returning to my Father and your Father, to my God and to your God'" (NIV). This little speech was directed to Mary Magdalene who remained near the tomb even after Peter and other disciples, whom she had told the news of the empty tomb and had brought to the tomb, left the scene. This passage is very important for the purpose of this paper particularly since Jesus describes that he will be *returning* to the Father, whose identity is clearly stated. Jesus' Father is also the Father of the disciples; he is also Jesus' God and the disciples' God. It is to him that

Jesus will return; after all, it is this Father who sent the son of man, namely Jesus, to below from above. Jesus descended and will ascend, having been lifted up onto the cross and glorified by the Father for having glorified him. This verse, therefore, can be seen as one that completes the son of man concept in the Gospel of John.

Furthermore, in light of the Sitz im Leben of the suffering Johannine community, Jesus' identification of his Father and God as his disciples' God and Father functions as an encouragement for the faithful, whom Jesus addresses as "my brothers," to remain persistent in their belief that Jesus, as the son of man, is the legitimate envoy of God. For just as Jesus returns to the Father, the faithful will follow after him at a later time (John 13:36).

Thus, members of the Johannine community, who chose to leave or were forced to leave the synagogue because of their belief in Jesus of Nazareth as the messianic envoy of God, derived their encouragement for continued faith from re-worked Johannine Christology with the term "son of man" confirming the legitimacy of Jesus of Nazareth through the imagery of heavenly origin and return, of being lifted up, and of being glorified. And John 3:13; 6:62; 8:28; and 20:17, texts examined closely in this paper, depict the integral role the term "son of man" with attached imagery plays within Johannine Christology. Indeed, the Johannine community was forced to define itself and survive; they had no other choice. To believe in Jesus of Nazareth as the messiah meant expulsion from the synagogue, the chief reference point of Jewish identity. Jewish Christians, therefore, came to find their identity with Jesus -- sharing the same Father, they became Jesus' "brothers."

Bibliography

Aland, Kurt, et al. *The Greek New Testament.* 3rd Ed. (Corrected). Stuttgart: United Bible Societies, 1983.

Ashton, John. *Understanding the Fourth Gospel.* Oxford: Clarendon Press, 1991.

Barrett, C. K. *The Gospel according to St. John.* London: S. P. C. K., 1972.

Bauer, Walter. *A Greek-English Lexicon of the New Testament and Other Early Christian Literature.* Rev. and aug. F. W. Gingrich and F. W. Danker from the Bauer's fifth edition. Chicago: The University of Chicago Press, 1979.

Cruden, Alexander. *A Complete Concordance to the Holy Scriptures of the Old and New Testament.* New York: M. W. Dodd, 1849.

de Jonge, Marinus. *Christology in Context: The Earliest Christian Response to Jesus.* Philadelphia: The Westminster Press, 1988.

Kittel, Gerhard (ed.). *Theological Dictionary of the New Testament.* Tr. and ed. Geoffrey Bromiley. Grand Rapids: WM. B. Eerdmans Publishing Company, 1964.

Martyn, J. Louis. *History and Theology in the Fourth Gospel.* Nashville: Abingdon, 1979.

Metzger, Bruce M. *A Textual Commentary on the Greek New Testament.* London: United Bible Societies, 1971.

Nickelsburg, George W. E. "Son of Man." *The Anchor Bible Dictionary* (Vol. 6). New York: Doubleday, 1992, pp. 137-150.

Painter, John. *The Quest for the Messiah: The History, Literature and Theology of the Johannine Community.* Nashville: Abingdon Press, 1993.

Schnackenburg, Rudolf. *The Gospel according to St. John.* London: Burns and Oates, 1980.

Holy Bible (New International Version). Grand Rapids: Zondervan Publishing House, 1989.

Self-Perception and Group Identity at Qumran: Hodayot Scrolls as a Key[1]

In the Mediterranean world in which dyadic personality was the chief expression of identity, the Qumran community found itself. Some scholars argue that there was an individualistic expression and identity at Qumran. They point to the Hodayot and their prominent "I" passages and textual content. Yet, an examination of the 1QH and 1QS texts, in light of their Sitz im Leben, shows that they serve as an insight into group identity. The individual perceived himself in light of his community.

Traditional societies tend to value community and group identity. Individuals not only see themselves in the context of the community in which they find themselves, they also tend to make it their business to

---

[1] I would like to thank Professor Daniel Schwartz of the Hebrew University of Jerusalem's Department of Jewish History for his helpful comments on this paper in 1994. I would also like to thank Professor Eileen Schuller of McMaster University of Canada, who was a visiting scholar at the Albright Institute in Jerusalem at that time for giving me two of her then unpublished papers for the benefit of my research into the Qumran community.

know the latest news about everyone in the community. When a person in the community does something unacceptable to the community protocol, he or she receives communal disapproval and dishonor. Many fear the judgment of the members of the community and act to maintain his or her honorable place within the community.

One can see such behavior in Korean villages of today. Everyone knows everything, and when a woman becomes pregnant before marriage, she is ostracized from the community. Everyone she sees throws comments denoting the position of shame in which she has come to within the community. Not only is this (dis)honor applied to her, but her whole family. One can see that an individual's value is provided by the collective judgment of the community based on the societal protocol to which the members of the community ascribes actively or passively. Such is the social matrix of traditional societies.

The Mediterranean world of the late Second Temple period was also traditional and, therefore, communal. Individual identity was integrally tied to group identity. Individuals behaved according to the honor-shame protocol of the community. Sociologically speaking, honor for a member in a traditional society is the approval of the community; shame, on the other hand, is the disapproval of the community. One feels shame or honor because he or she values the opinion of the others within the community. Honor and shame in this context is communally-binding; that is, other members in the community remind the member of his or her honor and shame. The sociological term to describe this perception of self and identity in light of the opinion of others in the community is dyadic personality. Dyadic personality was the chief reference for identity existent in the Mediterranean world of the late Second Temple. And it was in this environment that the Qumran community found itself.

Yet, some scholars assert that there was an individualistic pietistic expression and identity within the Qumran community and point to the Hodayot texts. Their argument hinges on two main points: content and grammar, especially the use of the personal pronoun of "I." Bilhah Nitzan is a major proponent of the thesis that the Hodayot express individualistic pietistic sentiment. Thus, one should perceive the Hodayot as thanksgiving songs of an individual rather than a liturgical prayer.[2] This is evidenced by the personal nature of the content of the Hodayot. First, the concrete nature of the experience in the texts points to the impact that sectarian problems had on the

---

[2] Bilhah Nitzan, *Qumran Prayer and Religious Poetry*, Tr. Jonathan Chipman (Leiden: E. J. Brill, 1994) 322-323.

individual who composed the Hodayot. The member expressed personal frustration for daily struggles with opponents; it was his way of venting his stress.[3] Secondly, the author of the Hodayot wrote down some individual theoretical reflections on the teachings of the sect. This, for Nitzan, shows that the Hodayot was written by an individual and represents a self expression. For, if the Hodayot had as their purpose group prayer, then they would not have had such sectarian nature. In prayers meant to be recited as a group, the members of the sect perceived themselves as a part of the congregation of Israel. Thus, commonality rather than differences were stressed.[4] Thirdly, these Hodayot are not a request or a supplication for forgiveness; rather, they are a personal reflection on the miracle of repentance given to such lowly creatures as humans and thanksgiving for God's kindness.[5] Nitzan argues that such element of reflection and theoretical speculation in the Hodayot are absent in prayers.[6] She gives 1QH xvi 4-16 as an example of "a theoretical-poetical expression of a certain mood."[7]

As one can see, personal nature of the Hodayot, such as the author's reflection

---

[3]Nitzan 324-5.
[4]Nitzan 332.
[5]Nitzan 337-8.
[6]Nitzan 342-342.
[7]Nitzan 340.

and experience, forms a foundational argument for Nitzan's thesis that the Hodayot were composed for an individualistic purpose and not for group prayers. This foundational argument finds commonality with the argument of Licht, Nitzan's *Doktorvater*. In the words of Nitzan, Licht argued that the Hodayot were "a personal practice of the poet and a mere literary habit."[8] This quote actually forms the main outline of her book. In her book, Nitzan tries to prove that the Hodayot express personal sentiments, that they are not prayers but songs, a form of poetry, intended as a personal outlet, rather than as a liturgy for the community. Thus, Nitzan writes:

> it is clear that the songs of the *Thanksgiving Scroll* are first and foremost poetic creations. .... On the other hand, those works intended to be recited by the congregation are generally speaking less poetic.... Many works of prayer are written predominantly in metric prose. This is the case in most of the works of prayer and thanksgiving in the *War Scroll*; in most of the *Blessings*; in the curses recited in the ceremony of initi-

---

[8]Nitzan 19.

ation into the covenant of the sect; in the blessing in 11QBer (=4Q285 1); in a number of songs in scrolls 4Q501-511; and in several of the fragments of the prayers of the festivals.[9]

One can see that Licht's opinion of the Hodayot functions as a catalyst for Nitzan's study of the Hodayot.

In her attempt to prove the individual poetic nature of the Hodayot, Nitzan does touch on important topics, as prayer and liturgy in the Second Temple period. She believes that fixed prayer originated in the Second Temple period and not after the Temple Destruction,[10] but in "no more than an initial step."[11] This fixity was first applied in regularity, or "liturgical table." Works that enumerate proper times for song and prayer to God are 11QPs^a (Psalms Scroll) xxxvii 2-11, 1QS x 1-8, and 1QH xii 1-11.[12] With time, fixity came to be applied to both content, or ideas, and form, or liturgy.[13] First sign of prayer formula that later took on a fixed shape appears in the prayer of praise in the Hebrew editions to

---

[9]Nitzan 345-346.
[10]Nitzan 14.
[11]Nitzan 44.
[12]Nitzan 9.
[13]Nitzan 115.

Ben Sira 51:12, which allude to the concluding formulae of the Eighteen Benedictions of rabbinic statutory prayer. Praises recited in the Ben Sira passage are: "to the redeemer of Israel"; "to the ingather of the dispersed Israel"; "to Him who built His city and His sanctuary"; "to Him who makes a horn to sprout for the House of David"; "to the shield of Abraham." In Nitzan's opinion, this suggests that these benedictions had already become customary during the time of the Second Temple, around the end of the third century BC., in oral form and in formulae that are not fixed.[14] It is Nitzan's opinion that such developments in fixed prayer existed for the "mainstream" Judaism and that the Qumran community did not isolate themselves from the prayer tradition that took shape parallel to the sacrificial cult.[15] Furthermore, Nitzan stresses the role of liturgical prayer in the Qumran community by stating that "the prayers of the people of Qumran became a form of divine worship equivalent to that of sacrifices."[16] But the Hodayot were not a part of this liturgical prayer tradition. They were personal songs to express personal reflection on the teachings of the community and frustration regarding sectarian conflicts. For, liturgical prayers stress commonality with the "main-

---

[14]Nitzan 41.
[15]Nitzan 115.
[16]Nitzan 115.

stream" Judaism and do not emphasize sectarian uniqueness as the Hodayot do.[17]

Svend Holm-Nielsen, on the other hand, argues that the Hodayot were examples of the Qumran community's liturgical prayers and songs of praise. Holm-Nielsen asserts that the Hodayot express the faith of the community but do not function as poems for instruction in dogmatics. The Hodayot are phrased in words of an individual, who is not a historical person, but rather represents the members of the community. This representative individual in the Hodayot describes his "assurance of salvation and fear of perdition in an existence where the battle lies between the power of God and the powers of Belial...."[18] The basis of this sentiment lies in the revelation that every member receives through the membership in the community. Thus, Holm-Nielsen believes that the Hodayot were most likely recited during the ceremony in connection with initiation into the community.[19]

Holm-Nielsen's arguments for the communal liturgical usage of the Hodayot lies in his understanding of their content and in his definitions of worship, cult, and liturgy. Holm-Nielsen asserts that the content of the Hodayot shows the community's self-

---

[17]Nitzan 354-355.
[18]Svend Holm-Nielsen, *Hodayot: Psalms from Qumran* (Aarhus: Universitetsforlaget I, 1960) 348.
[19]Holm-Nielsen 340-341.

awareness of being "the remnant of the people whom God has raised to life."[20] That is to say, the members of the Qumran community perceived themselves as the elect with whom God established a new covenant as the result of disregard of the old one by the majority of Israelites. Other documents from Qumran further corroborate the concept that not all children of Israel have the guarantee of salvation. The new covenant is for those who enter into it wholeheartedly, conforming to its conditions. Thus, revelation is only for the initiates of the community.[21] Revelation is important because it is one way to approach God and to influence one's own destiny; for God created the just and the unjust and ordained for them deliverance and destruction, respectively.[22] Besides this dualistic understanding of the world, the Hodayot also perceives humankind to be enslaved by sin; to be human is to sin. Thus, in essence, all human beings, even those created as the just, need God's revelation for salvation.[23] This is possible only through initiation into the Qumran community. Thus, it is no surprise that the Hodayot function as a liturgical prayer and songs of prayer in initiation ceremonies to affirm the members of the community as the

---

[20] Holm-Nielsen 284.
[21] Holm-Nielsen 283-4.
[22] Holm-Nielsen 281.
[23] Holm-Nielsen 274.

elect and the initiate as becoming a member of the Children of the Light.

Besides arguing for the liturgical use of the Hodayot through his examination of the content, Holm-Nielsen utilizes his definition of worship, cult, and liturgy to show the liturgical function of the Hodayot. Holm-Nielsen describes the terms and relationship among them in this manner:

> "Worship" and "cult" are, however, not identical for two reasons. For the first, the history of religion has to do with a cultic concept which is not based upon worship, but which is concerned with relationship to powers in existence which are not given the shape of actual gods. For the other, worship contains other elements than the cultic elements which can be included under the description, "liturgy." "Cult" and "liturgy" together form "worship." However, while "cult" is a primary concept, which is in itself not as yet "worship," "liturgy" forms the secondary concept coming at the point where there is a desire for fellowship. While the treatment of

"cult" may well be a matter for the individual, and even in certain forms be rendered impossible by the inference of others or even by their very presence, "worship" is a collective matter.[24]

Thus, cult and liturgy forms worship. But both elements do not necessarily have to be present to form divine worship. Even if a holy place must be abandoned, a holy ceremony can sanctify a place which is not already holy. Thus, the purpose of cult, which is to create and preserve holiness, can be achieved by liturgy.[25] According to Holm-Nielsen, this principle was evident in the post-exilic Judaism, in which worship was found not only in the Temple, but also in the synagogues.[26] The worship referred to here must point to liturgy, because sacrificial worship was performed at the Jerusalem Temple. One notes the common ground that Holm-Nielsen and Nitzan share -- namely, the concept that there was a parallel liturgical worship tradition that took shape alongside the sacrificial worship within the "mainstream" Judaism of the Second Temple period.

---

[24]Holm-Nielsen 333.
[25]Holm-Nielsen 333-4.
[26]Holm-Nielsen 335.

In the context of the Qumran community, the Hodayot were liturgy that functioned in place of the cult of sacrifice. To prove this, Holm-Nielsen points to 1QS 10:6ff. and especially the phrase, "the sacrifice of the lips," as showing that songs of praise took over the role of the sacrifice. In this sense, Holm-Nielsen is willing to accept the term, "spiritualized sacrifice," but prefers to see the songs of praise as a liturgical replacement of the missing cultic element of sacrifice.[27]

James Charlesworth agrees with the perception that the Hodayot played a crucial role in the worship tradition of the Second Temple period. Charlesworth argues that many hymns and prayers that were not included in the evolving canon of the so-called Old Testament were used authoritatively in Jewish services before and during the time of Jesus of Nazareth. Then, Charlesworth names the Hodayot as an example of an early sectarian hymn for which this holds true. Furthermore, Charlesworth warns against examining non-canonical texts with a theological bias or with a methodology different from those employed in the study of canonical writings.[28]

---

[27] Holm-Nielsen 346.
[28] James Charlesworth, "A Prolegomenon to a New Study of the Jewish Background of the Hymns and Prayers in the New Testament," *Journal of Jewish Studies*. xxxiii(1-2 1982, 265-285) 266-267.

If one takes Charlesworth's advice and examines the scholarship on canonical psalms, one notices that the predominant consensus is that these were used liturgically. It would not be totally wrong to say that Mowinckel's *Psalmenstudien* made the greatest impact on modern day psalm scholarship. Thereafter, large majority of scholars looked for a cultic situation to which each psalm may be assigned. In the 1960s Mowinckel came to allow for the existence of a dozen non-cultic psalms, which he called "learned psalmography" with members of his reconsturcted circles of the "wise" as authors. This reflects a change in his position of 1924 that there were two or three non-cultic psalms. But his fundamental position remained with the position that these non-cultic psalms as exceptions that prove the rule.[29]

Holm-Nielsen is less accepting of a position other than that all canonical psalms are cultic psalms. To achieve this end, Holm-Nielsen redefines the concept of "cultic psalms" to include not only pre-exilic psalms which belonged to ceremonial activities in the Temple but later psalms that came to be integral part of post-exilic synagogue services. For Holm-Nielsen, the term "psalm" by definition shows attachment to

---

[29]D. J. A. Clines. "Psalm Research since 1955: I. The Psalms and the Cult," *Tyndale Bulletin* 18 (1967, 103-126) 105-6.

divine service.[30] Here, Holm-Nielsen shows himself consistent with his thesis that the Hodayot, or the Thanksgiving Psalms from Qumran, were used liturgically in conjuncttion with a divine service, most likely the initiation ceremony.

In deed, Holm-Nielsen's argument for the liturgical usage of the Hodayot is strong. Not only does Charlesworth's proposed method of study of the Hodayot in light of canonical psalm research supports Holm-Nielson's thesis, even Nitzan's writing points to the strength of this thesis. In the beginning of her book, Nitzan considers three qualities in the Hodayot that are typical of works intended for worship: fixed introductory phrases, like "I will praise You, O Lord" or "Blessed are You, O Lord"; a fixed literary genre, namely, thanksgiving; and many hymnic phrases. It is interesting to note that Nitzan was only able to come up with two arguments in support of her thesis that the Hodayot were written by an individual for himself. These are the poet's use of "I" and his emphasis on his personal experiences.[31] Taken on face value, one may say that Nitzan does more harm to her thesis and supports Holm-Nielsen's argument.

Furthermore, Eileen Schuller's study of the cave 4 Hodayot, or 4QH, supports the idea that the Hodayot were intended for

---

[30]Clines 106.
[31]Nitzan 16.

liturgical use. First of all, the existence of multiple copies of the Hodayot points to group usage. There are eight copies of the Hodayot: 1QH^a, 1QH^b(=1Q35), and 4QH^{a-f}.[32] The force of this argument is enhanced by the fact that these copies range widely in date, as ascribed according to hand writing of the manuscripts. The earliest copy, 4QH^b, is from the Middle Hasmonian period, and most recent copies, 4QH^{d,e,f}, are from the Herodian period.[33] Second of all, 4QH^a provides a strong proof that the Hodayot were used liturgically by the Qumran community. Opponents of the liturgical usage of the Hodayot point to the prominent "I" passages, but 4QH^a provides "we" passages and weakens the proponents of the thesis that the Hodayot were individual compositions meant for the self. Schuller explains:

> However, in 4QH^a 7 there is a long fragment, forty lines in

---

[32] Eileen Schuller, "The Cave 4 Hodayot Manuscripts: A Preliminary Description," Annenberg Conference (1993, Unpublished Draft) 1. Thanks again to Professor Schuller for allowing me to use this unpublished paper.

[33] Eileen Schuller, "Thanksgiving Psalms from Cave 4 and the Hymnic Texts from Qumran," Notre Dame (1993, Unpublished Draft) 13. Thanks again to Professor Schuller for allowing me to use this unpublished paper.

two consecutive columns, which overlaps with several small fragments (46 ii, 56 ii, 55 ii, 7 ii) of 1QH whch in the reconstructed order of 1QH^a form col. xxvi. This hymn contains typical "I" hodayot language in the first stanza ("as for me, my rank is with the heavenly beings"), but moves to "we" language in the soteriological confession.... Similarly, another fragment in 4QH^a (frg. 3) overlaps with 1QH frg. 10 and enables us to read much more of this hymn in this first person plural "we sing out ... we recount ... you have instructed us."[34]

It is clear, based on the history of research on Hodayot, and current directions in research that there was a form of group identity based on a type of self-perception that can be understood in liturgical terms. Individualistic prayers at Qumran were performed as a group. A type of interchange of individualistic and group prayers indicates somewhat of confusion in term of religi-

---

[34]Schuller, "Thanksgiving Psalms from Cave 4 and the Hymnic Texts from Qumran" 13-14.

osity. What constituted individual prayers? What constituted group prayers, or prayers meant to be recited as a group? Why was there this confusion? All these questions help point the way further into research regarding individualism and group identity in Qumran.

Bibliography

Charlesworth, James. "A Prolegomenon to a New Study of the Jewish Background of the Hymns and Prayers in the New Testament." *Journal of Jewish Studies.* xxxiii (1-2 1982), pages 265-285.

Clines, D. J. A. "Psalm Research since 1955: I. The Psalms and the Cult." *Tyndale Bulletin* 18 (1967), pages 103-126.

Holm-Nielsen, Svend. *Hodayot: Psalms from Qumran.* Aarhus: Universitetsforlaget I, 1960.

Nitzan, Bilhah. *Qumran Prayer and Religious Poetry.* Translated by Jonathan Chipman. Leiden: E. J. Brill, 1994.

Schuller, Eileen. "Thanksgiving Psalms from Cave 4 and the Hymnic Texts from Qumran." Notre Dame (1993, Unpublished Draft).

Schuller, Eileen. "The Cave 4 Hodayot Manuscripts: A Preliminary Description." Annenberg Conference (1993, Unpublished Draft).

Continuity and Discontinuity in Christian Baptism[1]

Baptism was an essential element in the lives of the early Christians. But baptism itself was not the creation of the early Christian community. There was the baptism of John the Baptizer, which approximated Christian baptism most closely and, indeed, proceeded it. But the Johannine baptism, too, was not a creation *ex nihilo*. It found itself in the Jewish religious and cultural setting. Therefore, resemblances with Johannine baptism appear in Jewish lustrations, the proselyte baptism of the Pharisees, and the proselyte baptism of the Essenes and the Qumran community. But significant differences exist between the Johannine baptism and its Jewish parallels, as in the function of baptism, so that it would be wrong to say that Johannine baptism is a direct copy of contemporary or earlier Jewish baths. But to deny the similarities would be sheer folly for the historian. The Johannine baptism best resembles Christian baptism, which owes its birth to the baptism of Jesus of Nazareth in the

---

[1] I would like to thank Professor Scott Bartchy of UCLA for reading this paper and commenting on it.

Jordan River. Despite the resemblance, Christian baptism differs from Johannine baptism in that Christian baptism possesses a baptismal formula and has an active involvement of the Spirit of God. Furthermore, Paul of Tarsus ascribes the idea of the believer's mystical union with Christ in his death and resurrection to the event of Christian baptism. At first glance, one may think that Hellenistic religious culture -- especially the taurobolion of the cult of Attis -- influenced Pauline ideas of baptism. But a closer examination will show that this analogy is limited. Especially, the idea that Christian baptism unites all believers baptized in the name of Jesus of Nazareth to each other, as well as to Jesus, was a revolutionary idea, particularly because of the radical inclusivity that was attached to this idea.

    First, an examination of the Jewish background for baths would be appropriate for setting a foundation for comparing Johannine baptism with other Jewish baths. Resemblances of baptism are found in the Old Testament. One example of such a resemblance is found in the story of Naaman and Elisha in II Kings 5:1ff. Naaman, who was a commander in the army of the king of Aram, incurred leprosy. A servant girl, who served Naaman's wife said that if Naaman met Elisha, he would be healed. Thus, Naaman made a journey to Israel. When

Naaman came to the door of Elisha's house, Elisha sent him a message: "Go, wash yourself seven times in the Jordan, and your flesh will be restored and you will be cleansed" (II Kings 5:10 NIV). When Naaman obeyed this order, he was healed of leprosy. Here, one can see that a bath cleansed someone of an unclean illness.

The idea of a bath as a cleansing agent, indeed, came to play a more significant role in the lives of the Israelites. This is evident in the Jewish concept of lustration. Gerhard Barth writes:

> Das Alte Testament kennt eine Reihe von Fällen, in denen der Israelit sich rituell verunreinigt hat und deshalb seine kultische Reinheit durch festgesetzte Washung wiederherstellen muß: Berührung von Toten, Geschlechtsverkehr, Menstruation, Geburt, Aussatz und andere krankhafte Erscheinungen verunreinigen den Israeliten und ebenso der kontakt mit Menschen oder Gegenständen, die Träger dieser Unreinheit sind (1981:29).

Thus, one sees the important role lustration played in purification.

What were some of the characteristics of lustrations? First, these baths were not partial baths. One did not only wash a part of the body, but rather the whole body. Total immersion in water was involved. Second, these baths were performed by the individual on oneself. Third, these baths were done regularly. Fourth, these baths imparted cultic purity, but did not remit sins (29-30).

Beside lustrations, Pharisaic proselyte baptism played an important role in imparting ritual purity, though it did not remit sins. Barth writes:

> Denn beim Proselytentauchbad geht es nicht um Sündenvergebung, sondern um Vermittlung der kultischen Reinheit bzw. um Beseitigung der dem übertretenden Heiden als Heiden anhaftenden kultischen Unreinheit (30-31).

Both Jewish lustration and Pharisaic baptism imparted ritual purity, but the similarity between them stopped there.

Jewish proselyte baptism differed from lustrations in the way it was administered. Gilmore describes in his article

"Jewish Antecedents" found in the book he edited, *Christian Baptism*:

> But it must be remembered that proselyte baptism was more than 'another' lustration. It was an initiation ceremony, performed once only; it differed from other lustrations in that whereas they were performed in private, baptism took place before witnesses, being accompanyied by a catechism and a solemn exhortation; furthermore, lustrations were self-administered, and baptism was administered by others (1959: 66).

One can see the similarity of this proselyte baptism with Johannine baptism. Both were administered by another person. But, unlike Johannine baptism, proselyte baptism was normally administered with circumcision (Schnackenburg 1964:7).

There is some question, however, about the dating of proselyte baptism. This is an important question since the dating could have a direct bearing on the question of the dependence of Johannine or Christian baptism on Jewish proselyte baptism. Some date the origin of proselyte baptism around

65 AD. In "Jewish Antecedents," Gilmore describes this position and addresses the difficulty of dependence of Christian baptism on Jewish proselyte baptism:

> The difficulty arises from the fact that there is little or no evidence for the baptism of proselytes prior to A.D. 65, when the Jews pronounced all Gentiles unclean and baptism became essential for all Gentiles passing over to Judaism. It has been argued, therefore, that this is the origin of proselyte baptism, in which case it can only be an antecedent of Christian baptism if the institution of the latter be put quite late. (67).

But Gilmore's opinion is not an undebated one. In fact, Abrahams argues for the presence of proselyte baptism in the time of Jesus:

> Unnecessary doubt has been thrown on the prevalence of baptism as an initiatory rite in the reception of proselytes during Temple times. Schürer, while exaggerating the

number of ablutions prescribed by Pharisaic Judaism, rightly insists ... that both *à priori*, and from the implications of the Mishnah (*Pesahim*, viii. 8), proselytes must have been baptized in the time of Jesus (1967:36).

Whatever the dating might be, it is clear that baptismal practices resembling those of Johannine and Christian baptism existed in other Jewish sects.

The Essene community also had a proselyte baptism. Josephus' account of the Essene community shows that acceptance into the Essene community was a long process. Anyone who wanted to be a part of the Essene community had to wear a white linen habit and loin-cloth and carry a trowel during the first year of one's three year probation. At the end of the first year, the novice was allowed a ritual purification in water -- i.e. baptism. Two more years, however, had to pass before the novice was admitted to the communal meal (Bruce 1969:87).

Ritual purification in water was especially an important element for the Qumran community. Ritual washings, however, were not for the forgiveness of sins, but rather an intensification of the levitical laws concerning purity (Barth 32). This is in agreement with all other Jewish baths, except for Johannine Christian baptism. For the Qumran community, the priestly ritual wash came to have an extended force. Bruce describes: "... in fact, the special ablutions which the levitical law prescribes for the priests appear to have been prescribed at Qumran for all the members of the community" (108). Therefore, ritual bath was not merely an initiatory ceremony, but rather performed frequently (108).

Gerhard Barth believes that the Qumran water purification provided an example for the Johannine baptism because of the eschatological expectation and the intensification of the Law. He writes:

> Weiter meinte man, in den Waschungen der Qumran-Gemeinschaft, das bestimmende und auslösende Vorbild für die Johannestaufe finden zu können. Eschatologische Erwartung und Tora-Verschärfung (Beruf) verbinden zweifellos Qumran und den Täufer (32).

There are definite similarities between John the Baptizer and the Qumran community. But how similar was Qumran ritual purification and Johannine baptism? It is true that both had an element of eschatological expectation and that baptism was done in parallel to that expectation. The Qumran community believed their purity would prepare them to be used by God when the eschatological end came. John the Baptizer, resembling the Qumran community in its eschatological expectation, cried out: "Repent, for the kingdom of heaven is near" (Matthew 3:2 NIV).

There are, however, evident differences that preclude one from extending the analogy too far. For example, John the Baptizer practiced radical inclusivity in his baptism. One sees in the third chapter of Luke that John the Baptizer baptized everyone who was willing, including the tax collectors (verse 12) and the Roman soldiers (verse 14). This stands in stark contrast from the radical exclusivity and selectivity of the Qumran community.

Furthermore, Johannine baptism involved the remission of sin, and not merely administration of ritual purity. Thus, Luke writes in his gospel: "[John the Baptizer] went into all the country around the Jordan, preaching a baptism of repentance for the forgiveness of sins" (3:3 NIV). But, as noted earlier, the Qumran community, as well as all other major Jewish ritual washings, did not remit sin, but rather administered ritual purity. Also, Johannine baptism was a one-time ritual, in contrast to Qumran ritual washing that was repeated over and over again (Barth 37). Thus, one sees that there were similarities and differences between the Qumran ritual bath and Johannine baptism. But the similarities do not outweigh the differences to the extent that one could confidently say that the Johannine baptism is solely dependent on Qumran ritual bath.

Just as there is some similarity between Qumran ritual washing and Johannine baptism, the Pharisaic proselyte baptism does have some similarity with Johannine baptism. Both of them were administered by another person in front of witnesses. Abrahams comments: "The baptism by John resembles the baptism of proselytes in several points, among others in the fact that both forms of baptism are *administered*, not performed by the subject himself. At all events, the proselyte's bath needed witnessing" (38 Italics Not Mine).

But there are differences. First of all, John's baptism was done in the open, publicly, by the Jordan River, whereas proselyte baptism was done in private before witnesses (Gilmore 72). Also, Johannine baptism aimed at the forgiveness of sins, whereas proselyte baptism aimed at the ritual purity of the body. Abrahams describes the difference: "But there is, it is often said, this difference between Johannine and Pharisaic baptism: the former was a moral, the latter a physical purification" (39). Furthermore, Johannine baptism had a greater eschatological emphasis. John saw his baptism as marking the initiation into the new age. Johannine baptism, therefore, stands in contrast to proselyte baptism. Gilmore explains: "Proselyte baptism began and ended in time; John's baptism looked forward to the dawn of the Messianic age, and sought to prepare people for it" (73).

Thus, one can see that the Synoptic Gospel writers saw John's baptism activities in the desert as a fulfillment of Isaiah 40:3 (cf. Matthew 3:3; Mark 1:2f; Luke 3:4), which reads: "A voice of one calling: 'In the desert prepare the way for the Lord; make straight in the wilderness a highway for our God'" (NIV). The Gospel writer John even has John the Baptizer describing himself as the fulfillment of this passage to the priests and Levites who came to inquire who he was. It is written in the Gospel of John:

> Finally they said, "Who are you? Give us an answer to take back to those who sent us. What do you say about yourself?" John replied in the words of Isaiah the prophet, "I am the voice of one calling in the desert,

'Make straight the way for the Lord'" (1:22f).

Thus, one can see that the Messianic expectation was a crucial part of Johannine baptism. This eschatological expectation of Johannine baptism sets it in contrast with Pharisaic proselyte baptism.

Jewish lustrations, Qumran ritual bath and proselyte baptism have common elements with Johannine baptism. But many differences hinder one from asserting that Johannine baptism was completely dependent on them. But there is a closer bond between Johannine baptism and Christian baptism. In fact, von Campenhausen believes that they were not distinguishable at first: "Er meint, daß in der Anfangszeit die Christliche Taufe überhaupt nicht von der Johannestaufe unterschieden worden sei ..." (Barth 45). A study of the characteristics of Christian baptism will show the similarities which could lead one to make such a statement.

Christian baptism has many elements that correspond to Johannine baptism. Christian baptism finds similarity with Johannine baptism in the mode and frequency of baptism. Both were not self-administered, but rather administered by a baptizer. Also, both considered baptism as an initiation into the eschatological community, so baptism was administered only once. Barth describes: "Die christliche Taufe ist ebenso wie die Johannestaufe eine einmalige Handlung. Das folgt vor allem aus ihrem Charakter als Initiationsritus, durch dem der Täufling in die eschatologische Heilsgemeinde aufgenommen wird..." (37).

Furthermore, Christian baptism, as is with Johannine baptism, involves a change of heart in light of eschatological expectation. Barth writes: "Wie die Johannestaufe ist auch die christliche Taufe mit der Umkehr in eschatologischer Stunde verbunden. Es sind Umkehrende bzw. Glaubende, die zur Taufe kommen" (39).

Closely connected with the concept of the change of heart is the idea of baptism as remitting sins. Schnakenburg explains: "The Christian bath of cleansing stands both in contact and in contrast with the baptism of John. The washing away of sins indicates an area of common significance. The baptism of John also was a βαπτισμα μετανοιας (Acts xix. 4)..." (8).

And the remission of sins is a gift in both cases. The most visible sign of this is the passive nature of Christian and Johannine baptism. It is done to a person. Barth describes:

> Wie der Täufling nicht aktiv sich selbst tauft, sondern passiv die Taufe empfängt, so ist sein Tun nicht primär die

Erfüllung eines göttlichen Gebotes oder einer religiösen Leistung, sondern das Empfangen einer Gabe. Diese Gabe wird wie bei der Johannestaufe also Vergebung der Sünden bezeichnet (40).

One can see the similarities between Christian baptism and Johannine baptism. But differences do exist between Johannine and Christian baptism. The primary difference between them is the existence of a baptismal formula for Christian baptism. In Acts, Peter preaches, exhorting all to be baptized in the name of Christ for the forgiveness of sin: "Peter replied, 'Repent and be baptized, every one of you, in the name of Jesus Christ for the forgiveness of your sins'" (2:38a NIV). This stands in contrast with John the Baptizer's message of repentance which excludes any kind of baptismal formula. Luke describes in his Gospel accounts: "[John the Baptizer] went into all the country around the Jordan, preaching a baptism of repentance for the forgiveness of sins" (Luke 3:3 NIV). Schnackenburg agrees that the existence of a baptismal formula was the distinguishing element between Christian and Johannine baptism: "Over against the baptism of John the distinguishing mark of Christian baptism is its administration εις το ονομα του κυριου Ιησου ..." (8). Indeed, Paul is shown as having made that distinction himself when he was talking to some "disciples." It is written in Acts 19:3-5:

> So Paul asked, "Then what baptism did you receive?" "John's baptism," they replied. Paul said, "John's baptism was a baptism of repentance. He told people to believe in the one coming after him, that is, in Jesus." On hearing this, they were baptized into the name of the Lord Jesus... (NIV).

Thus, baptism in the name of Jesus distinguishes Christian baptism with Johannine baptism.
    This baptismal formula, however, poses some questions for the historian specializing in early Christianity. Baptism in the name of Jesus is a baptismal formula that is different from that which Jesus of Nazareth is recorded as having given to the eleven disciples on a mountain in Galilee. Matthew records the words of Jesus of Nazareth in his Gospel: "Then Jesus came to them and said, "All authority in heaven and on earth has been given to me.

Therefore go and make disciples of all nations, baptizing them in the name of the Father and of the Son and of the Holy Spirit ..." (28:18-19 NIV). The two baptismal formulae are evidently different. The former involves only the name of Jesus, but the latter includes the Trinity -- Father, Son, and the Holy Spirit. Some scholars believe that the Trinitarian formula ascribed to Jesus of Nazareth in Matthew is a later development. One such scholar is Gerhard Barth, who writes: "Aber dieser Taufbefehl in Mt 28,19 ist ein relativ später Text, dessen Überlieferung sich nicht bis in die erste Zeit nach Ostern oder gar ins Leben Jesu zurückverfolgen läßt" (13).

But unlike Conybeare, Barth feels that the baptismal formula ascribed to Jesus is a part of the Gospel of Matthew, rather than a later Christian interpolation. Barth writes:

> Schon die Formelhaftigkeit des bereits trinitarisch oder besser triadisch ausgestalteten Taufwortes läßt eine jüngere Entwicklung vermuten. Zwar dürfte das triadische Taufwort von der Abfassung des Matthäusevangeliums an zu seinem Text gehört haben und nicht erst, wie Conybeare meinte,

> eine spätere Interpolation sein (13).

As Barth writes, the triadic formula is a part of Matthew's writing.

This is evident when one examines the baptism of Jesus, as accounted by Matthew. It is written in Matthew 3:16f:

> As soon as Jesus was baptized, he went up out of the water. At that moment heaven was opened, and he saw the Spirit of God descending like a dove and lighting on him. And a voice from heaven said, "This is my Son, whom I love; with him I am well pleased" (NIV).

Here, one sees the presence of God the Father and God the Son in Jesus' baptism. Although John the Baptizer did not use a baptismal formula in baptism, Matthew describes the activity of God the Father and God the Spirit at Jesus' baptism. Thus, Barth is not incorrect in ascribing the triadic baptismal formula to the Gospel writer rather than to a later Christian interpolator.

Furthermore, Jesus' baptism marks a turning point from Johannine baptism to Christian baptism, thereby providing a distinction between them. Johannine baptism was merely a ritual for the forgiveness of sins, but Jesus' baptism was marked by a special quality -- the descent of the Spirit of God on Jesus of Nazareth that marked him as the Messiah, or the Lamb of God. The gospel writer John describes the testimony of John the Baptizer concerning Jesus of Nazareth:

> The next day John saw Jesus coming toward him and said, "Look, the Lamb of God, who takes away the sin of the world! This is the one I meant when I said, 'A man who comes after me has surpassed me because he was before me.' I myself did not know him, but the reason I came baptizing with water was that he might be revealed to Israel." Then John gave this testimony: "I saw the Spirit come down from heaven as a dove and remain on him. I would not have known him, except that the one who sent me to baptize with water told me, 'The man on whom you see the Spirit come down and remain is he who will baptize with the

Holy Spirit.' I have seen and I testify that this is the Son of God (1:29-34 NIV).

Thus, Jesus' baptism is important as a marker of the difference. Therefore, R. E. O. White comments in his article, "The Baptism of Jesus," found in the book edited by Gilmore: "The essential difference between John's version of proselyte baptism and Christian baptism as we met it in Acts *is* the baptism of Jesus" (84 Italics Not Mine).

Early church leaders recognized the difference between Christian baptism and Johannine baptism. One can see an example of this in Acts 19. While in Ephesus, Paul asked the disciples there whether or not they received the Holy Spirit when they believed. Upon their negative response, Paul asked which baptism they received. They had received Johannine baptism. Thus, Paul baptized them again, and, this time, in the name of Jesus. And when he laid his hands on them, they experienced the activity of the Spirit of God. Luke describes in Acts 19:6: "When Paul placed his hands on them, the Holy Spirit came on them, and they spoke in tongues and prophesied" (NIV).

Thus, after Jesus' baptism, Christian baptism became associated with the activity of the Spirit of God. When Peter exhorted all to repent and be baptized in the name of Jesus in Acts 2:38, it was after their experience with the Holy Spirit. Luke describes this experience in Acts:

> When the day of Pentecost came, they were all together in one place. Suddenly a sound like the blowing of a violent wind came from heaven and filled the whole house where they were sitting. They saw what seemed to be tongues of fire that separated and came to rest on each of them. All of them were filled with the Holy Spirit and began to speak in other tongues as the Spirit enabled them (2:1-4 NIV).

The association between Christian baptism and the activity of the Spirit of God is a running theme in Acts. Its significance is attested by the story of Cornelius and his household. When the Spirit came upon them, Peter perceived the legitimacy for baptizing them, although they were Gentiles. Luke gives account in Acts:

> While Peter was still speaking these words, the Holy Spirit came on all who heard the message. The circumcised believers who had come

> with Peter were astonished that the gift of the Holy Spirit had been poured out even on the Gentiles. For they heard them speaking in tongues and praising God. Then Peter said, "Can anyone keep these people from being baptized with water? They have received the Holy Spirit just as we have. So he ordered that they be baptized in the name of Jesus Christ (10:44-48a NIV).

Thus, one can see the intricate relatedness of the working of the Spirit of God with Christian baptism. Stanly explains in his article, "Baptism in the New Testament," found in the book edited by T. Worden: "In the case of Cornelius and his household, Peter saw that the coming of the Holy Ghost was proof of God's will that they should be aggregated to the apostolic community by Christian Baptism" (1966:56).

Christian baptism not only differed with Johannine baptism in its characteristic baptismal formula and in the active participation of the Spirit of God, but it was further set apart from Johannine baptism in the complexity of theology that formed around it.

Paul of Tarsus perceived baptism as more than a mere purification ritual or a remission of sin. Rather, Paul saw baptism as uniting the baptized mystically with Jesus of Nazareth in his death and resurrection. Thus, Paul writes in Romans:

> Or don't you know that all of us who were baptized into Christ Jesus were baptized into his death? We were therefore buried with him through baptism into death in order that, just as Christ was raised from the dead through the glory of the Father, we too may live a new life. If we have been united with him like this in his death, we will certainly also be united with him in his resurrection. For we know that our old self was crucified with him so that the body of sin might be done away with, that we should no longer be slaves to sin -- because anyone who has died has been freed from sin. Now if we died with Christ, we believe that we will also live with him (6:3-8 NIV).

Thus, Paul uses the idea that those who have Christian baptism participate in Jesus' death and resurrection; therefore, they should live life corresponding to Christian morality.

Some scholars have noted similarities between this idea of Paul's with the rites of the Hellenistic mystery cults. After all, Paul was within the context of Hellenized Mediterranean culture. A. J. M. Wedderburn comments: "Jewish Christians, including Paul, may have unwittingly taken over from their Graeco-Roman environment ideas and language that were shared by the mysteries and pagan religion..." (1987:163).

Wedderburn's comment is understandable when one examines the taurobolium in the cult of Attis and inscriptions related with it. Everett Ferguson describes the taurobolium:

> The person receiving the rite entered a deep underground pit that was covered with a wooden lattice work. A garlanded bull was brought to the planks covering the pit and killed with a spear. The blood ran through the openings and showered the initiates below, who held up his face so that the blood covered

it and so that he could drink some (1987:228).

When this rite was performed with a goat, it was called "criobolium." There are two types of inscriptions concerning the rite in the cult of Attis. Ferguson describes:

> ...most of the earlier ones pertain to a sacrifice, offered by individuals, associations, cities, or provinces for the welfare of the emperor, his household, his empire, or themselves; the later ones are predominantly acts of personal consecration (229).

The later inscriptions show resemblance to Pauline ideas of Christian baptism. The rite in the cult of Attis carried with it idea of purification, and a term like "reborn" is found among the inscriptions. Ferguson describes:

> The "initiatory" or "dedicatory" use of the rite probably carried the idea of a purification, perhaps in preparation for the afterlife. Hence, a few inscriptions speak of the person as "reborn," usually for a period of about twenty

> years, although one (CIL VI.510 from A.D. 376) speaks of the person as "reborn for eternity" (229).

This exhibits some similarity with Paul's idea of having new life by participation in the resurrection of Christ through baptism.

But an exaggerated comparison between the rites in the cult of Attis and the Pauline ideas associated with Christian baptism can be misleading. Helmut Koester states: "Many have speculated about the interpretation of the Attis mysteries, but we do not know whether they were related to the ideas of death and resurrection .... The myth never speaks about a resurrection of Attis" (1982:1:193).

Not only are there some questions concerning the similarity in ideas, but there also is a difference in the physical administration of the rites. Schnackenburg writes: "... *tauro-* or *criobolion* of the Attis worship was not a water but a blood baptism" (13). But there is a more fundamental difference that this implies. Unlike the rites of the cult of Attis, Christian baptism did not involve reenactment. Wedderburn writes: "The Christian rite of initiation, baptism, is ... no re-enactment of Christ's death and resurrection or ritual representation of the initiate's death and resurrection on the analogy of Christ" (378-9). Rather, Paul of Tarsus was describing a mystical union with Jesus in his death and resurrection.

Paul's ideas concerning union with Jesus of Nazareth in baptism was not merely on an individual level, but rather on a corporate level. All who are baptized in the name of Jesus have union with Christ. Thus, all who are part of the community of believers baptized in the name of Jesus must live in harmony. So, Paul of Tarsus writes strongly against the factions that existed in the Corinthian church:

> I appeal to you, brothers, in the name of our Lord Jesus Christ, that all of you agree with one another so that there may be no divisions among you and that you may be perfectly united in mind and thought. My brothers, some from Chloe's household have informed me that there are quarrels among you. What I mean is this: One of you says, "I follow Paul"; another, "I follow Apollos"; another, "I follow Cephas"; still another, "I follow Christ." Is Christ divided? Was Paul crucified for you? Were you baptized into the name of

Paul? (I Corinthians 1:10-13 NIV).

It is evident that baptism in the name of Jesus makes one a member of a unified and harmonious community of believers. Stanly comments: "In Paul's view, the unity of the Church derives from the personal union with Christ entered into by each Christian at his Baptism" (59).

For Paul, therefore, unity of the believing community must transcend racial, social, and sexual boundaries. Paul of Tarsus writes: "The body is a unit, though it is made up of many parts; and though all its parts are many, they form one body. So it is with Christ. For we were all baptized by one Spirit into one body -- whether Jews or Greeks, slave or free ..." (I Corinthians 13:12f NIV). Paul again writes in his letter to the churches in Galatia: "You are all sons of God through fath in Christ Jesus, for all of you who were baptized into Christ have clothed yourselves with Christ. There is neither Jew nor Greek, slave or free, male nor female, for you are all one in Christ Jesus" (Galatians 3:26-28 NIV). Unlike the exclusive mystery religions, such great emphasis in unity was radical in the context of Paul's time, and, thus, it provided a distinctive mark for Christian baptism and its implications over against all other resembling baths.

In conclusion, Christian baptism is a tradition that has been carried out for nearly two millennia. In an attempt to understand the origin and the significance of Christian baptism, it is important to examine similar rites ingrained in the historical context of Christian baptism. Jewish religion provides lustrations and proselyte baptisms which have resemblances with Johannine baptism, the direct precedent of Christian baptism. But there are differences between Johannine baptism and other Jewish baths -- especially in the idea of the extent of efficacy -- that hinder one from claiming that any one of the Jewish baths is that from which John the Baptizer copied.

Jesus' baptism by John the baptizer marked the beginning of Christian baptism, with activity of the Spirit of God associated with it. But there are differences between Johannine baptism and Christian baptism, like the existence of a baptismal formula for the latter. Furthermore, Paul of Tarsus forwards the idea of the unity of the believer with Jesus in his death and resurrection at Christian baptism. At a first glance this seems to have resemblances to the rite of the cult of Attis, but upon closer examination, one can see that this provides no direct precedence to Christian baptism and the ideas Paul ascribes to it. Furthermore, Christian baptism and Paul's concept of radical unity of the believers through baptism in the name of Jesus sets Christian baptism apart from all that resemble it.

Bibliography

Abrahams, I. 1967. *Studies in Pharisaism and the Gospels*. New York: Ktav Publishing House, Inc.

Barth, Gerhard. 1981. *Die Taufe in frühchristlicher Zeit*. Neukirchen-Vluyn: Neukirchener Verlag.

Bruce, F. F. 1969. *New Testament History*. New York: Doubleday.

Ferguson, Everett. 1987. *Backgrounds of Early Christianity*. Grand Rapids, Michigan: William B. Eerdmans Publishing Company.

Gilmore, A. (ed.). 1959. *Christian Baptism*. London: Lutterworth Press.

Koester, Helmut. 1982. *Introduction to the New Testament (Volume 1): History, Culture, and Religion of the Hellenistic Age*. New York: Walter de Gruyter & Co.

Schnackenburg, Rudolf. 1964. *Baptism in the Thought of St. Paul*. Tr. G. R. Beasley-Murray. Oxford: Basil Blackwell.

Wedderburn, A. J. M. 1987. *Baptism and Resurrection.* Tübingen: J. C. B. Mohr (Paul Siebeck).

Worden, T. (ed.). 1966. *Sacraments in Scripture.* London: Geoffrey Chapman Limited.

1984. *The Holy Bible: New International Version.* Colorado Springs, Colorado: International Bible Society.

John Calvin's Views on Government[1]

John Calvin was a very interesting man, to say the least. Often referred to as the "pope of Geneva," this French reformer strove to achieve in Geneva, Switzerland, his idea of the ideal state. Yet, Calvin was not a mad-man who controlled the city of Geneva merely with his charisma; on the contrary, Calvin worked with a systematic political philosophy which he intelligibly and logically introduced in the *Institutes*. Although many ideas of Calvin from the section "On Civil Government" in the *Institutes* seem almost a duplication of Luther's writings, a closer examination shows Calvin's writing to be more developed and organized. Calvin uses the Bible as his chief authority in coherently describing the origin, nature, and functions of government.

Calvin's political views are shown in the *Institutes*, and especially through his chapter "On Civil Government," one can see that Calvin was too much of a genius to be

---

[1] I would like to thank Professor Claus-Peter Clasen of UCLA's History Department, a world renown expert on the Reformation, for his helpful comments on this paper and his active encouragement.

regarded as a fanatic. His systematic opinion is derived from the Bible. This is no more evident than in Calvin's treatment of the origin of civil government. Not unlike Martin Luther, John Calvin shows the origin of civil government as from God. There is, however, a slight difference in the way they support their arguments. Luther primarily used Peter and Paul as supporting the divine origin of secular government, but Calvin refers to Jesus Christ to support his thesis. This is shown in Calvin's explanation of the title "gods" in Psalm 82:1, 6, which is applied to magistrates:

> When all who sustain the magistracy are called "gods," it ought not to be considered as an appellation of trivial importance, for it implies that they have their command from God, that they are invested with his authority and are altogether his representatives, and act as his vicegerents. This is not an invention of mine, but the interpretation of Christ, who says, "If he called them gods, unto whom the word of God came, and the Scripture cannot be broken." What is the meaning of this but that their

commission has been given to them by God, to serve him in their office...?[2]

Thus, by quoting Jesus Christ from John 10:35, John Calvin uses the most respected man in the Christian Europe of his times to legitimize his argument.

On the premise of the divine origin of civil government, Calvin encourages strict obedience to civil authority, even in the case in which the ruler is a tyrant. Calvin writes that tyrants "...ought to be regarded by his subjects, as far as pertains to public obedience, with the same reverence and esteem which they would show to the best of kings, if such a one is granted to them."[3] Calvin supports this with a scripture passage from Jeremiah 27:5-9, 12. In this passage, the king of Babylon is called "my servant" by God, and the reader is exhorted through the passage to "Therefore serve the king of Babylon and live." To Calvin, this undoubtedly shows the importance of being submissive even to a tyrant. In this passage, God had commanded that "all nations" serve a "cruel tyrant, for no other reason than that he possessed the kingdom." Calvin points out one must view his present government in

---

[2]John Calvin, On God and Political Duty, ed. John T. McNeill (New York: Macmillan Publishing Company, 1950) 48.
[3]Calvin, 75.

light of this passage. Thus, one must be submissive to a government, regardless of its quality.[4]

This stance of Calvin has prodded many scholars to comment. Some scholars have tried to interpret Calvin's stance in a sociological way. One such scholar is Georgia Harkness. She feels that the reason for Calvin's espousal of non-resistance as a God-given duty is that the political climate had changed. The Calvinist state of Geneva was slowly being established, and it was expedient for Calvin to teach people submission to the civil authorities. Thus, Harkness comments:

> Two types of political environment foster a promotion of the doctrine of non-resistance as a religious duty. When a new religion is weak and must rely for its existence on the favor of the established powers, it preaches submission. When it becomes strong and dominates the political situation itself, it again preaches submission. Only in the intermediate stage, when it is strong enough to rebel but not to dominate, is it likely to

---

[4]Calvin, 77.

encourage resistance. Nor is it through any conscious opportunism or compromising of its message that a religious emphasis adjusts itself to political circumstance. It is rather through the subtle psychological processes of rationalization which so often make theory conform to expediency without the possessor's recognizing that he is advocating the expedient.[5]

In essence, Harkness held that subconscious "situation ethics" influences religious thinkers in general, and influenced Calvin in particular. Willem Balke also interprets Calvin's writing in light of Calvin's social atmosphere, although at a slightly different level. Balke feels that Calvin wrote with the Anabaptists primarily in mind -- a kind of "we are not like *them*" apologetics for the Reformed and against his "primary foe," the Anabaptists. Balke writes, "Calvin is greatly concerned to point out in this chapter that

---

[5]Georgia Harkness, John Calvin: The Man and His Ethics (New York: Henry Holt and Company, 1931) 224.

the Reformed people sincerely honored the government as God's servant."[6]

Both Harkness and Balke interpret Calvin's views on civil government primarily from sociological standpoint. This has its merits. For all things occur in a sociological framework. Yet, it has its dangers, too. For instance, it is more than reasonable to say that the political situation of the times affected John Calvin, but they miss the mark in seeing John Calvin's philosophical standpoint. He was a man highly educated in the humanist tradition, who had wrested himself away from that tradition to the tradition of what can be loosely called the *sola scriptura* position of the Reformation. This was not merely an intellectual move, but also a revamping of personal philosophy in light of his new-found convictions. Thus, Calvin argued from his convictions founded on the Bible. This is why one sees in the *Institutes* numerous Biblical examples arranged by Calvin in a systematic way. It would not be fair for one to say that Calvin was primarily guided by his social situation. Rather, Calvin's religious philosophy prompted Calvin to discuss civil government in this way. It was not merely an apologetic treatise against the Anabaptist, although one would not doubt that the

---

[6]Willem Balke, Calvin and the Anabaptist Radicals, trans. William Heynen (Grand Rapids, MI: William B. Eerdmans Publishing Company, 1981) 60.

Anabaptist factor had played an important role. Wilhelm Niesel tries to assess Calvin from a theological perspective. Niesel writes,

> Thus when Calvin teaches that civil government was instituted of God, he is not thinking of an ill-defined supernatural foundation of human rules but of the one Lord Jesus Christ. The kingdoms of this world are grounded in Him and maintained by Him. .... All magistrates and princes are therefore bidden to subject themselves in all humility to the great king Jesus Christ and to His spiritual sceptre. Their government can be nothing other than a service under this one Lord.[7]

For the historian, this statement, at first glance, may seem too extreme. Yet, one has to keep in mind the point of view from which Calvin argued. Niesel understands that perspective. Although Calvin seems to argue for political absolutism, one can see

---

[7] Wilhelm Niesel, <u>The Theology of Calvin</u>, trans. Harold Knight (London: Lutterworth Press, 1956) 231-232.

that Calvin places civil authority below God. Calvin writes, "The Lord, therefore, is the King of kings; who, when he has opened his sacred mouth is to be heard alone, above all, for all, and before all; in the next place, we are subject to those men who preside over us but no otherwise than in him."[8] Thus, Calvin leaves room for resistance. One is to obey his authority even if it is unjust or tyrannical, but when authority goes against God and his wishes, one has to obey God rather than man. Calvin likens government to a parent or a husband. Even if they are harsh, one is bound by Scriptures to obey them, as long as they are not going against God.[9] These examples are in keeping with scriptural premises. Ephesians 6:1-4 talks about the duty of children to parents. Verse 1 states, "Children, obey your parents in the Lord, for this is right." (NIV) The only qualification to obedience is the phrase "in the Lord." This is later expounded on by Paul in verse 4. It states, "Fathers, do not exasperate your children; instead bring them up in the training and instruction of the Lord." Although there is a clause of warning to parents, there is no justification found in the passage of disobedience except an implied one in the case where parents are not "in the Lord." The passage about obedience to husbands is found in Ephesians

---

[8]Calvin, 81.
[9]Calvin, 78.

5:22-33. Particularly of interest are verses 22-24. Paul writes, "Wives, submit to your husbands as to the Lord. For the husband is the head of the wife as Christ is the head of the church, his body, of which he is the Savior. Now as the church submits to Christ, so also wives should submit to their husbands *in everything*" (NIV, *Italics Mine*) Wives are to submit to their husbands at all times, but there is also the underlying qualifying notion of Christ as being the chief authority -- for, both husband and wife, who compose the church, come under the ultimate authority of Christ.

One sees why Calvin used the notion of obedience to parent and husband as a parallel to obedience to civil authorities. They are ideal models for showing Calvin's concept of submission to authority. In fact, the Shorter Catechism drawn up by Calvinists and accepted and taught by Reformed Churches (Orthodox Presbyterian Church, Presbyterian Church in America, Ko-shin Presbyterian Church, Hap-dong Presbyterian Church, to name few modern denominations) shows the fifth commandment of obedience to father and mother as an encompassing command for all authority. Thus, question number 65 in the catechism asks, "What is forbidden in the fifth commandment?" and the answer is "The fifth commandment fobiddeth the neglection of, or doing any thing against, the honour and duty which belongeth to every one in their several places and relations."[10] Yet, G. I. Williamson, in his commentary to the Shorter Catechism, explains that disobedience to authority is permissible when that authority goes against God. Thus Williamson writes, "We see, then, that there will be times when *Christians will have to resist the abuse of God-given authority.* .... It is not Christian to break laws merely because we do not like them. The Bible clearly teaches that resistance is legitimate only at that point where the authority is transgressing the scriptural limits."[11] This shows that G. I. Williamson is in keeping with Calvin's beliefs.

John Calvin goes on to discuss the nature and functions of civil government. In describing the nature of civil government, Calvin emphasizes the vitality of its existence in society. Thus, Calvin writes that civil government "...is equally as necessary to mankind as bread and water, light and air and far more excellent."[12] Furthermore, Calvin criticizes those who use their "liberty" that Christ gave to annul the institution of government, but he also criticizes the other extreme in which some allocated to

---

[10] G. I. Williamson, The Shorter Catechism: For Study Classes (Volume 2) (New Jersey: Presbyterian and Reformed Publishing Company, 1970) 51.
[11] Williamson, 53-54. *Italics Not Mine*
[12] Calvin, 46.

rulers absolute power on the premise of the divine institution of civil government. Calvin writes in a strong language:

> ...infatuated and barbarous men madly endeavor to subvert this ordinance established by God, and, on the other hand, the flatterers of princes, extolling their power beyond all just bounds, hesitate not to oppose it to authority of God himself. Unless both these errors be resisted, the purity of the faith will be destroyed.[13]

One can see Calvin's effort at a balanced position.

But Calvin distinguishes the difference between the spiritual world and the physical world, as Luther did. Calvin states that those who belong to the spiritual world, namely Christians, have no need of laws in the ultimate sense since they have the internal reign of Christ. Not only that, they are experiencing a prelude to heaven, in which there would be one authority, namely that of Christ Jesus. But as human beings live in this imperfect world, civil governments are needed.[14]

---

[13]Calvin, 44.
[14]Calvin, 45-46.

Calvin identifies three forms of government -- monarchy, aristocracy, and democracy. He names the dangers of all these governments. Monarchy could lead to despotism, aristocracy to oligarchy, and democracy to sedition. All forms of civil government could be corrupted. Calvin prefers a mixture of aristocracy and democracy in a civil government, in which there is mutual assistance and admonition. But, Calvin concludes by saying that "...if it be his pleasure to appoint kings over kingdoms, and senators or other magistrates over free cities, it is our duty to be obedient to any governors whom God has established over the places in which we reside."[15] Here, like Luther, Calvin quotes Paul who said in Romans 13 that "there is no power but of God" and also Peter who exhorts in I Peter 2:13-14, 17, "honor the king" as reasons why one must submit to authority,[16] besides other arguments already discussed in the beginning part of this paper.

Closely tied with Calvin's discussion of the nature of civil government is Calvin's concept of the two part composition of society: those who make, uphold, and rule with laws; and those who are ruled by laws. Law is the linking factor. Thus these three elements -- ruler, the ruled, and the law -- must be properly understood, according to

---

[15] Calvin, 54.
[16] Calvin, 52.

Calvin. Calvin writes, "But the perspicuity of order will assist the reader to attain a clearer understanding of what sentiments ought to be entertained respecting the whole system of civil administration, if we enter on a discussion of each branch of it."[17] Calvin felt that these "branches" needed to work harmoniously. One scholar holds that this concept is crucial in understanding Calvin's view of civil government. This scholar, W. Stanford Reid, explains that the Old Testament concept of the covenant explains this harmonious process. Thus, he writes, "Calvin's whole pattern of political thinking is brought together in his concept of the covenant. ...the medieval view that rulers and subjects are linked together by mutual contract, and above everything else, the biblical example of Israel's covenant with God, led him to adopt this interpretation."[18] Thus, Reid explains that both rulers and the ruled have responsibility under a Calvinist political system.

The subject's responsibility, as noted before, is obedience. The civil government also has responsibilities. This is expounded on by Calvin on his discussion of the fun-

---

[17] Calvin, 47.
[18] W. Stanford Reid, "Calvin and the Political Order," John Calvin, Contemporary Prophet, ed. Jacob T. Hoogstra (Philadelphia: The Presbyterian and Reformed Publishing Company, 1959, pp. 243-257) 249.

ctions of civil government. Here, Calvin's ideas show a greater sophistication than Luther's. Calvin divides the responsibilities into two major areas -- for God and for men. Thus, Calvin comments,

> ...this civil government is designed, as long as we live in this world, to cherish and support the external worship of God, to preserve the pure doctrine of religion, to defend the constitution of the Church, to regulate our lives in a manner requisite for the society of men, to form our manners to civil justice, to promote our concord with each other, and to establish general peace and tranquility....[19]

There are two things which would be well to remember as one considers the religious duty of the government. First of all, it is in keeping with the premise of Calvin that civil government originates from God. Logically speaking, if government originates from God, it naturally has a duty to him. Secondly, one must keep in mind that Calvin was addressing a "Christian" audience. This concept was not altogether foreign to his

---

[19] Calvin, 46.

audience which had experienced a "corrupted" version of it through Roman Catholicism. This fact prompted John T. McNeill to comment, "...he is addressing Christian rulers and subjects of professedly Christian states, and is of course primarily concerned with politics in a Christian setting."[20]

In discussing civil government's duty to God, Calvin shows his concern for this topic. As an introduction to his argument, John Calvin comments that even the heathen government sees fostering of piety to a deity as its first object. Thus, Christian magistrates must be ashamed if they ignore this facet of their function. Calvin writes, "If the Scriptures did not teach that this office extends to both tables of the law, we must learn it from heathen writers; for not one of them has treated of the office of magistrates, of legislation, and civil government without beginning with religion and Divine worship."[21] Then, Calvin goes on to argue that God gave the greatest commendation to those rulers in the Bible who devoted their attention to the growth of religion and who restored the worship of God when it had been corrupted or abolished.[22] Calvin be-

---

[20] John T. McNeill, "Calvin and Civil Government," Readings in Calvin's Theology, ed. Donald K. McKim (Grand Rapids, MI: Baker Book House, 1984, pp. 260-274) 265.
[21] Calvin, 54.
[22] Calvin, 54.

lieves in this so much that he speaks in a strong language against those who oppose this view:

> These things evince the folly of those who would wish magistrates to neglect all thoughts of God, and to confine themselves entirely to the administration of justice among men, as though God appointed governors in his name to decide secular controversies, and disregard that which is of far greater importance....[23]

Thus, one can see the importance Calvin attributed to the religious functions of civil government to oversee sacred and proper worship of the God of the Bible.

John Calvin does not neglect the civil functions of government, however. As with Luther, Calvin sees civil government as promoter of peace and maintainer of justice. Thus, Calvin writes that the civil magistrates are appointed to be:

> ...the protectors and vindicators of the public innocence, modesty, probity, and tranquility, whose sole object

---

[23] Calvin, 55.

it ought to be to promote the common peace and security of all. .... But as they cannot do this unless they defend good men from the injuries of the wicked and aid the oppressed by their relief and protection, they are likewise armed with power for the suppression of crimes, and the severe punishment of malefactors whose wickedness disturbs the public peace.[24]

To maintain peace and render justice, Calvin, as Luther, feels capital punishment to be a legitimate tool. Calvin believes that when a magistrate sentences someone to death, it is ultimately a judgment of God, so it is justified. It is not, at all, "to hurt" or "to destroy," which would be ungodly, but, rather, it is avenging the afflictions of the righteous.[25] And Calvin goes on further to cite Moses who slaughtered three thousand men who had committed idolatry as recorded in Exodus 32:26-28. Also, David commanded Solomon to put Joab and Shimei to death in I Kings 2:5-9. Calvin assesses these two examples, "Both Moses and David, in executing the vengeance com-

---

[24]Calvin, 56.
[25]Calvin, 57.

John Calvin's Views on Government

mitted to them by God, by this severity sanctified their hands, which would have been defiled by lenity."[26] Then, Calvin gives a warning to civil magistrates to be wary of falling into either of the extremes of being too severe or too lenient.[27]

In keeping with the function of civil governments to maintain peace and justice, Calvin justifies "righteous" war. Calvin gives three reasons why the legitimacy of war is still applicable. First, Calvin says that the reasons for going to war in the ancient time as now have not changed. It would be for defense, in the case of a just war. So the legitimacy of war is still applicable. Secondly, the argument that war is not lawful due to the silence of the Apostles is a poor argument in Calvin's eyes. To Calvin, war was not abrogated. Apostles did not mention war because they were not interested too much in organizing civil government. So the ancient approval of war would still be applicable. Thirdly, there is a great implication that no change occurred in the New Testament in the concept of war. Here, Calvin quotes Augustine, who commented that if wars were unlawful, then John the Baptist would have told soldiers to quit their jobs. Instead, John the Baptist had told them in Luke 3:14 to be "content" with their

---

[26]Calvin, 58.
[27]Calvin, 59.

wages.[28] But Calvin is cautious to check an alacrity for war. Calvin writes, "But here all magistrates ought to be very cautious, that they follow not in any respect the impulse of their passions."[29]

Besides the treatment of capital punishment and war, Calvin addresses another factor that concerns justice and public well-being -- namely, litigation. Calvin argues that it is a good thing to turn one's cheek as Christ commands, but if litigation is necessary for maintaining peace for the public or others, litigation is legitimate.[30] Furthermore, Calvin states that the reason why Paul exhorted the Christians at Corinth not to bring cases before a secular court is that there was excessive litigation and it was defaming Christianity in the pagan world.[31] But if one fosters no feeling of revenge or hostility, but rather justice, then there is nothing wrong with litigation. Thus, Calvin writes, "...judicial processes are lawful to those who use them rightly...."[32] And overseeing litigation is one of the functions of civil government.

John Calvin, thus, has well thought-out views on the origin, nature, and functions of civil government. But the meticu-

---

[28]Calvin, 60.
[29]Calvin, 61.
[30]Calvin, 69.
[31]Calvin, 70.
[32]Calvin, 67.

lousness of Calvin is further evidenced in his provision for the financial support of civil government and magistrates. Thus, Calvin writes, "In the last place, I think it necessary to add that tributes and taxes are the legitimate revenues of princes; which, indeed they ought principally to employ in sustaining the public expenses of their office, but which they may likewise use for the support of their domestic splendor which is closely connected with the dignity of the government that they hold."[33] Even here, Calvin supports his view with examples of David, Joseph, Daniel, who lived at public expense.

From beginning to end, Calvin uses Biblical passages, examples, and allusions to support his argument. His systematic presentation of the origin, nature, and functions of civil government is supported by Scripture. Thus, one would have to approach his writings from that perspective to really comprehend the intricacies and the genius of Calvin's writing. When one approaches Calvin's writings with unfounded prejudices and a mere socio-political perspective, he will never enjoy the beauty of Calvin's religio-philosophical writings placed in the socio-political setting.

---

[33]Calvin, 61.

Bibliography

Balke, Willem. Calvin and the Anabaptist Radicals. Trans. William Heynen. Grand Rapids, MI: William B. Eerdmans Publishing Company, 1981.

Bouwsma, William J. John Calvin: A Sixteenth-Century Portrait. New York: Oxford University Press, 1988.

Calvin, John. On God and Political Duty. Ed. John T. McNeill. New York: Macmillan Publishing Company, 1950.

Harkness, Georgia. John Calvin: The Man and His Ethics. New York: Henry Holt and Company, 1931.

McNeill, John T. "Calvin and Civil Government." Readings in Calvin's Theology. Ed. Donald K. McKim. Grand Rapids, MI: Baker Book House, 1984, pp. 260-274.

Niesel, Wilhelm. The Theology of Calvin. Trans. Harold Knight. London: Lutterworth Press, 1956.

Reid, W. Stanford. "Calvin and the Political Order." John Calvin, Contemporary Prophet. Ed. Jacob T. Hoogstra. Philadelphia: The Presbyterian and Reformed Publishing Company, 1959.

Williamson, G. I. The Shorter Catechism: For Study Classes (Volume 2). New Jersey: Presbyterian and Reformed Publishing Company, 1970.

-------------- The Holy Bible (New International Version). New York: New York International Bible Society, 1978.

Luther's Position on War[1]

Having been surrounded by rebellions and wars, Martin Luther took a strong position on war. Basing his arguments on the Scriptures, Luther took the position that war had been instituted by God for justice, protection, and peace. To justify his position regarding war, he expounded on the concept of secular authority and its functions in the society. Also, Luther writes about the nature and function of soldiers -- those who actually fight war under secular authority. Yet, Martin Luther's approval of war is no way indicative of simple-mindedness nor a war-loving nature. For Luther carefully elaborates on three cases -- overlords fighting subjects, equals fighting equals, and subjects fighting overlords.

Martin Luther is quite emphatic in his position that war had been instituted by God for justice, protection, and peace. Thus, Luther writes,

> God be praised for that! For the very fact that the sword

---

[1] I am grateful to Professor Claus-Peter Clasen of UCLA's history department for his encouragement and helpful comments on this paper.

has been instituted by God to punish the evil, protect the good, and preserve peace is powerful and sufficient proof that war and killing along with all the things that accompany wartime and martial law have been instituted by God. What else is war but the punishment of wrong and evil? Why does anyone go to war except because he desires peace and obedience?[2]

Luther's position is thus more than clear on this.

But to get to this point, Luther first used several scriptural passages to support the legitimacy of Secular Authority. Luther claims that secular authority is a divine institution. He uses two of the most revered men in the Scriptures at his time, namely Paul and Peter, to prove his claims. Luther quotes Paul in Romans 13 in which Paul wrote,

"Let every soul be subject to the governing authority, for there is no authority except from God; the authority which everywhere exists has

---

[2]"Whether soldiers, Too, Can Be Saved," Luther's Works, Volume 46, Fortress Press: Philadelphia, 1967, p. 95.

been ordained by God. He then who resists the governing authority resists the ordinance of God and he who resists God's ordinance will incur judgment"³

Luther further quotes Peter as approving secular authority: "Be subject to every kind of human ordinance, whether it be to the king as supreme, or to governors, as those who have been sent by him to punish the wicked and to praise the righteous."⁴ And in Peter's statement, one can see the role of the secular authority. It exists for the punishment of the wrong-doers, offenders of society, threat to society, and for the reward or protection of good citizens by providing peace.

Then, Luther expounds on the form of punishment. Luther legitimizes the use of "sword" for punishment; thus, capital punishment is seen as a legitimate form of punishment by a secular authority. He quotes Paul's Romans 13 for this: "The governing authority does not bear the sword in vain. It is God's servant for your good, an avenger upon him who does evil."⁵ By

---

³"Temporal Authority: To What Extent It Should Be Obeyed," <u>Luther's Works, Volume 45,</u> Fortress Press, Philadelphia, 1962, pp.85-6.
⁴"Temporal Authority," p. 86.
⁵"Temporal Authority," p. 99.

using this passage from the New Testament, Luther shows that the Old Testament concept of capital punishment has not been negated in the New Testament and post-New Testament era. For there were those who were confused by the paradox between the concept of capital punishment as it existed in Old Testament laws and the seeming abrogation of that by Jesus Christ in Matthew 5 in which he encourages, "Do not resist evil, but make friends with your accuser...." and by Paul in Romans 12, "Vengeance is mine, I will repay, says the Lord."[6] Furthermore, Luther shows that the concept of punishment by "sword" was a law set from the beginning of the world -- before the Mosaic Law -- for all men. Thus, Luther retells the story of Cain's murder of Abel and subsequent events. According to Luther, the reason why Cain was afraid for his life and God had to place for him special protection from death is that Cain heard from Adam that murderers are to be slain.[7] Luther thus exerted great effort to show the divine nature of secular authority and its role as peace-keeper and also avenger of wrongdoers, even by means of the "sword."

Martin Luther's attention to secular authority is crucial in the light of his support of war. For Luther, if the "sword" was a legitimate way to punish an individual then

---

[6]"Temporal Authority," p. 81.
[7]"Temporal Authority," p. 86.

it was also a legitimate "justice-tool" to punish groups of individuals and to maintain peace for the good and the "righteous." Martin Luther thus writes,

> If one punishes a thief or a murderer or an adulterer, that is punishment inflicted on a single evildoer; but in a just war a whole crowd of evildoers, who are doing harm in proportion to the size of the crowd, are punished at once. If, therefore, one work of the sword is good and right, they are all good and right, for the sword is a sword and not a foxtail with which to tickle people.[8]

Thus, Luther states that a just war is a tool with which to punish groups of wrongdoers.

In accordance with his idea that war is a tool for justice, Luther shows soldiers to be deliverers of justice. First of all, Luther shows that being a soldier is not a wrong thing. He cites the example of John the Baptist's encounter with soldiers. When asked by the solders what they should do, John the Baptist did not encourage them to stop doing what they were doing. Rather, according to Luther, John the Baptist en-

---

[8]"Whether Soldiers, Too, Can Be Saved," pp. 98-9.

couraged them in Luke 3 to "Rob no one by violence or by false accusation, and be content with your wages."[9] Luther claims, therefore, that John the Baptist praised being a soldier but condemned the abuse. Luther took it even further by saying that soldiers were tools of justice for God. Thus, Luther writes, "For the hand that wields this sword and kills with it is not man's hand but God's; and it is not man, but God, who hangs, tortures, beheads, kills and fights. All these are God's works and judgments."[10] And also a little bit more explicitly, Luther writes in "Temporal Authority": "For those who punish evil and protect the good are God's servants and workmen."[11] Thus, by giving credit to the office of soldiery, Luther gives support for war.

Martin Luther, however, does not possess a love for war. He is aware of the dangers that are involved in his approval of the principle of war. Thus, he states that war, in of itself, is good, but if those involved are bad, then the justice of war could be tainted. Thus, Luther exhorts, "we must see to it that the persons who are in this profession and who do the work are the right kind of persons, that is, godly and upright, as we shall hear."[12]

---

[9]"Whether Soldiers, Too, Can Be Saved," p. 97.
[10]"Whether Soldiers, Too, Can Be Saved," p. 96.
[11]"Temporal Authority," p. 100.
[12]"Whether Soldiers, Too, Can Be Saved," p. 94.

Luther further shows that he dislikes wars but only sees them as necessity. He divides society into two groups -- those belonging to the kingdom of God and others belonging to the kingdom of the world. Those belonging to the kingdom of God do not need the sword or secular law or wars because they would do everything out of love and with the Holy Spirit in their heart. But those who belong to the kingdom of the world need the sword so that they would not act without fear of punishment. And this world could never have all those who belong to the kingdom of God so that secular authority has to remain in order to maintain peace.[13] And although it is wrong to start a war, when people are threatened by an attack, the authorities of the attacked have the obligation to maintain peace by getting involved in a war. Luther thus writes,

> If people were good and wanted to keep peace, war would be the greatest plague on earth. But what are you going to do about the fact that people will not keep the peace, but rob, steal, kill, outrage women and children, and take away property and honor? The small lack of peace called war or the sword

---

[13]"Temporal Authority," pp. 89-92.

Luther's Position on War

must set a limit to this universal, worldwide lack of peace which could destroy everyone."[14]

Thus, Luther shows that he is not simple-minded about war, but rather, thoughtful about it. Moreover, Luther's caution and thoughtfulness is evident in that Luther comments on different kinds of war -- namely, when subject wage war against overlords, when equals wage war against equals, and when overlords wage war against subjects. First, Luther writes that subjects should not wage war against overlord and he refers to Romans 13 for support. He shows his displeasure in tyrannicide, which Romans had practiced. Instead, Luther introduces five ideas relevant to this issue. Luther fist points out that the overlords can only damage the physical elements, such as property and body, of the subjects and not the soul. And in the process of practicing cruelty to their subjects, overlords "damn their own souls." Secondly, however one looks at it, a wicked tyrant is better than any war. For when a mob is let loose, there is no telling what would happen. There is also more damage and death in war. Thirdly, God has the ability to kill tyrants, but he only allows

---

[14]"Whether Soldiers, Too, Can Be Saved," p. 96.

them to exist in order that the wicked will be punished. Fourthly, since this world is full of those who do not belong to the kingdom of God, there is always a threat that those people would rise up against the ruler according to God's will and decree. Fifthly, God can also raise up foreign rulers against the tyrant. In sum, the principle of "Vengeance is mine, says the Lord" applies here, and accordingly, Martin Luther dissuaded subjects from rising up and causing "unnecessary" war and break of peace.[15]

Now, the war of "equal versus equal" lay close to Martin Luther and his desire for peace. He thus starts out in the treatment of this topic with these words, "At the very outset I want to say that whoever starts a war is in the wrong."[16] Luther reminds that the governments have been instituted to maintain peace and not to start wars. Luther, therefore, proposes that wars should only be fought defensively for the sake of peace. And those who fight defensively will have God on their side. But Luther warns that even those fighting for peace and justice must not depend on justice, but rather on God for deliverance and victory.[17] Luther

---

[15] "Whether Soldiers, Too, Can Be Saved," pp. 103-110.
[16] "Whether Soldiers, Too, Can Be Saved," p. 118.
[17] "Whether Soldiers, Too, Can Be Saved," pp. 118-125.

thereby shows his caution in the matter of war.

In discussing the last type of war -- war waged by overlords toward subjects -- Luther still shows his wish that war could be avoided and peace be kept. Thus, Luther addresses both the overlords and the subjects. To the overlords, Luther reminds that they exist as authority appointed by God not for their own sake, but rather for the sake of the community. Thus, they are to have the support of the community and, in that light, bear the sword. To the subjects, Luther shows that the rulers would only practice fairness and show justice if everything between them and the subjects is in good order. But, Luther states that it is proper to fight subjects when they rebel.[18] Thus, Luther is in keeping with his premise that authority is established by God.

In his writings concerning war and issues related with it, Martin Luther is very cautious. Basing his arguments on the Bible, Luther constantly refers to the concept of secular authority established by God for justice and peace. Although Luther supports the idea of war, he, in no way, encourages it. Furthermore, Luther is careful to place God at the top of the authority structure. Thus, Luther writes that when a soldier knows a ruler to be in the wrong, he must not participate in the war since God is

---

[18]"Whether Soldiers, Too, Can Be Saved," pp. 125-6.

the prime authority.[19] But in accordance with his acknowledgment that war is an instrument of God's justice, Luther encourages soldiers to give their best in a just war. He writes, "When the battle begins and the exhortation of which I spoke above has been given, they should commend themselves to God's grace and adopt a Christian attitude."[20] Thus, conclusively, Luther in his writing concerning war focuses on the principle of *Sola Gratia* and *Sola Scriptura*.

---

[19]"Whether Soldiers, Too, Can Be Saved," p. 130.
[20]"Whether Soldiers, Too, Can Be Saved," p. 133.

About the Author

Heerak Christian Kim is a Visiting Professor of Biblical Studies at Asia Evangelical College and Seminary in Bangalore, India. He has held many prestigious fellowships, including the Raoul Wallenberg Scholarship (1995-96) and the Lady Davis Fellowship (1996-97), and has written many important academic books, including *Hebrew, Jewish, and Early Christian Studies: Academic Essays* and *Jewish Law and Identity: Academic Essays*.

www.ingramcontent.com/pod-product-compliance
Lightning Source LLC
Chambersburg PA
CBHW021839220426
43663CB00005B/316